The Trailblazer's Playbook

SYLVIA ACEVEDO

The Trailblazer's Playbook

**PRACTICAL TACTICS TO
RISE AGAINST THE ODDS
AND
ACHIEVE EXCELLENCE**

WILEY

Copyright © 2025 by John Wiley & Sons. All rights reserved, including rights for text and data mining and training of artificial intelligence technologies or similar technologies.

Published by John Wiley & Sons, Inc., Hoboken, New Jersey.
Published simultaneously in Canada.

No part of this publication may be reproduced, stored in a retrieval system, or transmitted in any form or by any means, electronic, mechanical, photocopying, recording, scanning, or otherwise, except as permitted under Section 107 or 108 of the 1976 United States Copyright Act, without either the prior written permission of the Publisher, or authorization through payment of the appropriate per-copy fee to the Copyright Clearance Center, Inc., 222 Rosewood Drive, Danvers, MA 01923, (978) 750-8400, fax (978) 750-4470, or on the web at www.copyright.com. Requests to the Publisher for permission should be addressed to the Permissions Department, John Wiley & Sons, Inc., 111 River Street, Hoboken, NJ 07030, (201) 748-6011, fax (201) 748-6008, or online at http://www.wiley.com/go/permission.

The manufacturer's authorized representative according to the EU General Product Safety Regulation is Wiley-VCH GmbH, Boschstr. 12, 69469 Weinheim, Germany, e-mail: Product_Safety@wiley.com.

Trademarks: Wiley and the Wiley logo are trademarks or registered trademarks of John Wiley & Sons, Inc. and/or its affiliates in the United States and other countries and may not be used without written permission. All other trademarks are the property of their respective owners. John Wiley & Sons, Inc. is not associated with any product or vendor mentioned in this book.

Limit of Liability/Disclaimer of Warranty: While the publisher and author have used their best efforts in preparing this book, they make no representations or warranties with respect to the accuracy or completeness of the contents of this book and specifically disclaim any implied warranties of merchantability or fitness for a particular purpose. No warranty may be created or extended by sales representatives or written sales materials. The advice and strategies contained herein may not be suitable for your situation. You should consult with a professional where appropriate. Further, readers should be aware that websites listed in this work may have changed or disappeared between when this work was written and when it is read. Neither the publisher nor authors shall be liable for any loss of profit or any other commercial damages, including but not limited to special, incidental, consequential, or other damages.

For general information on our other products and services or for technical support, please contact our Customer Care Department within the United States at (800) 762-2974, outside the United States at (317) 572-3993 or fax (317) 572-4002.

Wiley also publishes its books in a variety of electronic formats. Some content that appears in print may not be available in electronic formats. For more information about Wiley products, visit our web site at www.wiley.com.

Library of Congress Cataloging-in-Publication Data is Available:

ISBN: 9781394318919 (Cloth)
ISBN: 9781394318926 (ePub)
ISBN: 9781394318933 (ePDF)

Cover Design: Paul McCarthy
Cover Image: © Getty Images | Torn Paper: Miragec | Pathway: Bill Koplitz

SKY10121972_071725

*To Janet, Angelica, Mario, and Armando:
Steadfast and bound by love.*

Contents

Prologue: From a Dirt Street to the C-Suite — ix
Introduction: When You Find Out You're a Trailblazer — xi

Chapter 1   Convince Yourself: The Power of Clarity   1

Chapter 2   Create Opportunity: The Power of Courage   17

Chapter 3   The Three Nos: The Power of Conviction   39

Chapter 4   When Everything Shatters   59

Chapter 5   Picking Up the Pieces   77

Chapter 6   Succeeding at Failing   93

Chapter 7   Forgiveness   111

Chapter 8   Turning Point to Take Off   129

Chapter 9   Building Trust   151

Chapter 10   The Door Opens from the Inside   175

Acknowledgments   189
About the Author   193
Index   195

Prologue

From a Dirt Street to the C-Suite

My family lived on a dirt desert road in Las Cruces, New Mexico, at the time, a small rural town of less than 30,000 people, where the unrelenting sun paints the sky with fire and the horizon feels both limitless and impossibly out of reach. This is where my story begins—not in a sleek boardroom, not in the legendary halls of NASA, but in a cramped rental house on a dirt road, its walls barely sheltering a family of five. My mother, born in Mexico, and my father, from El Paso, Texas, worked hard every day to make ends meet. For a time, we didn't even have a home of our own, crowding eleven people—yes, eleven—into my Aunt Alma and Uncle Sam's modest house with just one bathroom to share.

Life was challenging. Our dirt-lined neighborhood became the epicenter of one of the final meningitis epidemics in the United States, and tragedy struck close to home. The virus tore through the community, claiming lives and shattering families. My baby sister, Laura—a vivacious toddler with boundless potential—was only 19 months old when she became gravely ill. Her fever soared, leaving indelible scars on her brain that altered her future and reshaped our family forever.

My parents, still in their twenties and overwhelmed by the weight of circumstances they couldn't control, found themselves drifting apart, consumed by their individual grief and uncertainty. As they struggled, we were left to confront a daunting reality: mourning the past while finding a way to survive.

But here's the twist: those dirt roads, those sleepless nights, that relentless fight for survival—they were not my story's end. They became my launchpad. From that dusty town, I found the fuel to aim higher than anyone imagined. That grit carried me to NASA, where I became a rocket scientist. It propelled me to Stanford University, where I became one of the first Hispanics—male or female—to earn a graduate degree in engineering. It launched me into Silicon Valley, where I climbed from the engineering ranks to executive roles in some of the most iconic tech companies. And it prepared me to lead on the national stage as a White House Commissioner in Education, as CEO of the Girl Scouts of the USA, and now, as a corporate board director for two cutting-edge public technology companies.

Now, imagine that little girl, her sneakers worn from walking dusty streets, her world framed by challenges—dirt roads, a life-altering health crisis, and financial struggle. Would you have looked at her and seen a future rocket scientist? A tech executive? A CEO? A corporate leader? In a time when girls and women were expected to dream only within the confines of teaching or nursing, how did I dare as a young girl to imagine something so vastly different? And how did I continue to foster the ambition to live a life of my potential?

The Trailblazer's Playbook is more than my story. It's a distillation of the transformative behaviors and mindsets that propelled me from that dirt street to the C-suite. It's a guide for anyone yearning to shatter limits and unlock their full potential. As you turn the pages, I'll share the hard-earned lessons, pivotal moments, and bold actions that transformed my life—offering insights to help you see your own journey in a new light and unlock your path to transformation.

Introduction

When You Find Out You're a Trailblazer

It's a funny thing to say out loud. Objectively, looking back with age, wisdom, and lots of accomplishments, I never thought of myself as a trailblazer. I mostly thought of myself as a determined woman, a girl from a dusty town in New Mexico, determined to chart a different path for myself. If I'm being honest, when my publishers recommended this title, *The Trailblazer's Playbook*, I was surprised. But I'm getting ahead of myself. Let's start when I realized I wasn't just a spirited, smart, and determined girl desperate to prove everyone wrong and defy the odds of what was expected and possible for girls, especially girls who looked like me.

On an unremarkable day in the mid-2000s, my phone started ringing, and being it was the early 2000s, I of course picked up the call without knowing who was calling. In a million years, I never would have guessed who it would be. On the other end was a researcher from Stanford University, her voice curious yet matter of fact. She explained that she was studying the university's engineering alumni and had come across my name. "Did you know," she asked, "that you were among the first Hispanics—male or female—to earn a graduate engineering degree from Stanford? I'd like to know how you did it."

Her words stopped me in my tracks. Just how was it that I was learning this so many years later from a random Stanford researcher? There was no one in my classes who looked like me, but I never would have considered that perhaps I was among one of the first ones. And to the point, her question seemed straightforward, but it was anything but simple. How did a young girl from Las Cruces, New Mexico—a place worlds away from Stanford's polished halls and recruiting networks—end up at one of the most prestigious engineering programs in the world? How had I navigated a path strewn with obstacles to compete and thrive among the brightest minds, many of whom had resources and privileges far beyond anything I'd known? That answer took years to unravel and process and is what I hope to share with all of you in this book.

I didn't wake up one morning saying I'm going to Stanford. I couldn't even place Stanford on the map. Initially, I didn't even have a plan. I had simply moved forward, one step at a time, driven by an unrelenting vision of what might be possible.

That phone call triggered something deeper. It became the spark for a journey of reflection, a process of tracing back through the moments, decisions, and lessons that had carried me forward. It also lit a fire of purpose in me—not just to celebrate what I had achieved but to share what I'd learned, so others might dare to reach for goals that felt just as far out of reach.

The power of that purpose hit me one day after a talk I gave at a California community college. As I stepped outside, I saw a long line of students waiting. Thinking it was the lunch line, I chuckled and turned to the event organizer. "That must be the line for lunch!" I said. She smiled and corrected me. "That's not the lunch line. That's the line of students who want to meet you."

In that moment, I saw it clearly: my story wasn't just mine—it was a source of inspiration for others. It was proof that audacious dreams could be realized, even by those starting from a place of hardship. That realization led me to write *Path to the Stars (Camino a las Estrellas)*, a memoir for middle schoolers, to scale my message beyond the one-on-one conversations. Its impact surpassed my expectations; the book has become a timeless guide for students and educators, showing how resilience, courage, and relentless effort can open doors to extraordinary futures.

But this new book, *The Trailblazer's Playbook*, takes what I have learned a step further. It isn't just a memoir—it's a guide for those who aim to live lives of profound potential, for those who are determined to break barriers, redefine expectations, and create meaningful change. It's a journey of defying expectations, persevering even after experiencing one of life's cruelest traumas, and believing in the strength of one's dreams—especially in fields like STEM, where my trailblazing career broke through barriers to open doors for others. *It's about holding yourself to higher expectations than what the world holds for you.*

As I speak to professionals across industries, the same question arises: "How did you break through in careers where no one looked like you? How did you keep going when the path seemed impossible?"

The answer lies in the key mindsets and strategies I share in this book. These are not generic self-help principles—they are hard-won lessons forged through personal struggle, professional setbacks, and the relentless pursuit of excellence. They are for those who yearn for more and are ready to act boldly, the innovators who refuse to settle for mediocrity, and the leaders who know that their potential is greater than the expectations the world has placed on them.

This book is for you. If you're ready to aim higher, push harder, and chart a path toward your boldest aspirations, *The Trailblazer's Playbook* is your guide to make it happen. Let's start the journey together. Dream Big. Act Boldly.

1 Convince Yourself

The Power of Clarity

It started as a simple question, asked during a conversation with the Stanford researcher in the mid-aughts: Why did I excel in math and science? At the time, I didn't have an answer. It felt natural to say, "I just liked it." But looking back now, I see it wasn't that simple. My success was rooted in pivotal moments from my childhood—moments that shaped my belief in myself before anyone else did.

Convincing yourself is the first and, perhaps, hardest step. It is far easier to accept the world's expectations for you, especially when they're set low. For me, this first step took shape in a desert town, in the shadow of a father's attention I desperately craved.

My mother was very strict, but her love was always abundant, warm, and unconditional. However, my father's love and approval were harder to earn. His praise wasn't freely given, and the yearning for his love and approval instilled in me a powerful motivation to excel, to prove myself worthy of his acknowledgment. It was through this pursuit that I began to carve out my identity, reinforcing a sense of self-worth and determination that would shape my path forward.

I grew up in a very traditional household. My parents, Ofelia Monge Acevedo and Benito Manuel Acevedo, met in El Paso, Texas, at a church social at the First Spanish Baptist Church. They were young adults when they started their family: first Mario, then two years later, I was born, followed by my sister Laura four years later, and then my brother Armando eight years later.

My father, a college graduate who had an ROTC scholarship from Texas Western College (now UTEP), fulfilled his military commitment by serving in the Army, first on active duty and then in the reserves. I was born while he was stationed at Ellsworth Air Force Base in South Dakota, a world far from the Chihuahuan Desert of the arid Southwest where my parents felt at home.

After my father's tour of service was over, our family moved to Las Cruces, New Mexico, bringing us closer to our roots in the Southwest and for a time, when my father couldn't find work, to live with other family members.

After my father got a job at White Sands Missile Range, we moved our family of five, two adults and three children, to a rental house on a dirt street in Las Cruces, New Mexico. My father, a traditional family patriarch, favored my older brother Mario—a dynamic that ignited a fierce competitive spirit within me as I craved my father's attention and set out to excel in everything that Mario did that my father valued, whether it was schoolwork, reading, or even firing pistols. Mario had a natural talent for reading, art, and model airplane building—interests that my father didn't nurture. But in subjects my father really cared about, reading, math, and science, I was determined to match, if not surpass, my brother.

My father, a dedicated reader of books and magazines, would often spend evenings at the small adobe building that housed the Thomas Branigan Library, just a short walk from our home. I longed to join him and my older brother on their library visits, anticipating the day I could explore that world alongside them. One evening, my brother returned home with a stack of books and proudly showed off his new library card. Instantly, I wanted one too, but my father was hesitant, unsure if I was responsible enough to care for borrowed books as someone who wasn't even in first grade.

Determined, I asked what I needed to do so I could have my own library card. My father set a condition: I could have one if I saved five dollars, enough to cover any possible damages or losses. Although this requirement hadn't been applied to my brother, it offered me a clear path forward to obtain the coveted library card. I threw myself into the pursuit of earning every coin, taking on extra chores, checking vending machines, and looking for any coins, whatever I could find to fill my piggy bank. One day, my mother agreed that my piggy bank felt heavy enough to hold at least five dollars. Together, we cracked it open, and I carefully counted the stacks of pennies, nickels, dimes, and the occasional quarter. To my delight, I had surpassed the five-dollar goal.

My mother took me to the local Doña Ana Bank, where I opened a savings account and received a savings passbook. That evening, when my father came home, I could hardly contain my excitement as I proudly showed him my passbook, proof that I had met his challenge. My father, holding my new savings passbook, finally agreed to take me to the library along with my older brother. We went to the library and later, as I held my very own library card in my hands, I realized something powerful: if I set a goal, worked hard, and didn't give up, I could achieve it.

Paid to Save Money

At the time, I didn't fully grasp the significance of being the only one in my family with a savings account. We lived entirely on cash, stretching each paycheck to make ends meet. A checking or savings account wasn't part of our world—it simply wasn't how we operated. Yet, without realizing it, my parents had already given me a foundation in hustle, discipline, and financial independence.

My father lived in the world of books and science, not finance, so it wasn't surprising that it was my mother who took me to the bank. My mother understood that even though she and my father didn't have a bank account or a credit card, the act of opening one for me, her eldest daughter, was a step toward something bigger. My mother saw a future for me where I could have choices, security, and the ability to shape my own financial destiny.

Once I had the savings passbook, I wanted to fill the rest of the pages. I still remember the thrill of adding a few more dollars to my account and handing my passbook to the bank teller. She entered my deposit—but then, on a separate line, added another amount. Confused, I asked what it was. With a smile, she explained that it was interest—money the bank paid me just for keeping my savings there. Even better, she said the more I saved, the more the bank would add each month. She told me that when I had saved $500—an astonishing sum for me at the time, a hundred times my initial deposit—she told me I could open a CD (certificate of deposit), where the bank would pay me even more interest. That moment wasn't just a lesson in financial literacy—it set me on a trajectory of disciplined saving, a principle that helped me reach my financial goals throughout my life. That small moment, that first deposit, planted a seed. It showed me that wealth wasn't just about what you earned—it was about what you saved, *and didn't spend,* so that it grew over time.

It was a lesson I carried forward, shaping my belief in what was possible. Later, I realized that small triumphs like this were lessons and preparation for much bigger dreams.

Family Heartbreak

Even though the streets in our neighborhood were unpaved, I didn't see it as a hardship—I saw it as home. I never thought about what we didn't have or that most families were just getting by. What mattered was the energy of the neighborhood—kids always outside playing, and a park just a few blocks away where every day felt like an adventure. There was a tiny corner store where a single penny could buy a piece of candy, and shelves conveniently stocked with basic food necessities. To me, it wasn't about what we lacked—it was about the fun and simple joys that were waiting just outside our front door.

But one day, everything changed. A meningitis epidemic swept through our dirt-road community, leaving heartbreak in its wake—shattering families, altering futures, and claiming far too many children's lives. My younger sister, Laura, just 19 months old, was among its victims. Her fever soared to dangerous heights, and when the fever finally broke, the damage was done—irreversible brain damage that would alter the course of her life forever. She would never be able to read beyond a first-grade level, her world now shaped by limitations that blindsided our entire family, changing everything in an instant.

Laura had been the spark of our family, a whirlwind of energy who lit up every room she entered. Determined to keep up with my brother and me, she had skipped the crawling stage entirely, launching straight into walking as if she couldn't wait to chase after life. But after the illness, everything shifted. Laura's life trajectory changed, as did our family's. Though she recovered physically and always had an engaging personality, her abilities were forever impacted, and we struggled to adjust to this new reality.

We were thrust into an unfamiliar world, one where love and resilience were tested in ways we never saw coming. But it wasn't just the challenges ahead—it was us. The foundation of our family had shifted, altered by the weight of grief, uncertainty, and the unspoken struggles that followed. We weren't just navigating a new reality; we were a different family now, forever changed.

My father carried on, going to work each day to provide for our family, as if nothing had changed. But for my mother, everything had. Shaken by the realization that the epidemic had only spread in our dirt-road neighborhood, she became determined to move us somewhere safer—a neighborhood with paved streets.

Until Laura's illness, my very traditional father had resisted the idea of my mother learning to drive. But I will never forget the moment she sat across from him at our green Formica kitchen table and, in a tone that left no room for argument, told him she had already signed up for driving lessons. And that once she had her license, the first thing she was going to do was find us a new home. She was resolute—she would protect her family and make sure Mario and I had access to better schools, opportunities we couldn't find where we lived.

That conversation was a turning point. I didn't have the words to explain it at the time, but I could feel it—something had shifted between my parents in a way that couldn't be undone.

My father was reluctant to leave the familiar neighborhood, but my mother was determined. With the help of Uncle Sam Barba, she discovered that my father qualified for a GI Loan, thanks to his military service. That changed everything. We weren't just moving—we were becoming homeowners for the first time.

Our new neighborhood had paved streets, neatly spaced houses, and an air of stability that should have been reassuring. But moving in the middle of the school year made everything feel foreign. The houses stood farther apart, the familiar hum of Spanish was replaced with English, and the tight-knit rhythm of our old community was gone. My brother Mario adapted more easily, making new friends, but I felt unmoored—a quiet sense of loss. Though I couldn't fully understand it then, I knew that our family—and my sense of safety—had been irrevocably altered.

I didn't have the words for it at the time, but I could feel the shift. The new streets were smoother, but life itself had changed in ways I couldn't yet grasp. The better school and bigger house couldn't erase the reality that nothing would ever feel familiar again. Laura's illness had been a breaking point, but the weight my mother carried and the unspoken changes between my parents made it clear—there was no going back. Our lives had taken a turn, and the world I had known was gone.

Teachers Matter

Initially, I disliked my new school, Alameda Elementary. Everything about it felt foreign—the routines, the faces, the expectations. I longed for the comfort of my old school, Bradley Elementary, where I had first discovered my love of learning. But without realizing it, my time in the national Head Start pilot program at Bradley had given me an unexpected advantage.

My Head Start teacher at Bradley Elementary, Mrs. Davenport, had quickly recognized that arts and crafts didn't hold my interest. Instead of forcing me to follow the standard activities, she encouraged me to bring my library books to "show and tell," where I could share the adventures I had read with my classmates. For the first time, I felt the thrill of storytelling, of bringing words to life, of holding an audience captive through the power of reading. Mrs. Davenport was the first person outside of my mother who saw something in me—who directly encouraged me to be and do my best. That early confidence would prove invaluable in my new school, though I didn't know it yet.

At Alameda, my teacher, Mrs. Miller, had a strict and structured approach to her classroom. She stack-ranked students based on academic performance—those closest to her were the top achievers, while those in the back struggled the most. It was an unspoken hierarchy, but every student understood what it meant. When I joined the class, Mrs. Miller moved my desk to the end of the very last row. The student in front of me turned around and said, "Now you are the dumbest one in the class." His words stung. I already felt like an outsider in this new school, and now, according to the unspoken rules of Mrs. Miller's seating chart, I had been labeled the lowest of the low. I really didn't like Alameda Elementary.

However, soon after I started at the school, Mrs. Miller had the class take turns reading aloud from the *Weekly Reader*. When it was my turn to read aloud, I could feel the eyes of everyone in the classroom on me, the new girl who was seated in the last row in the class. But as I read, the words flowed effortlessly, just as they had when I shared stories at Bradley. When I finished, Mrs. Miller looked up, nodded approvingly, and then, to my surprise, stood up from her desk. Without a word, she walked over, lifted my desk, and moved it closer to the front—closer to her desk. The entire class watched in stunned silence.

That moment shifted something in me. The unfamiliar environment, the paved streets, the sense that life had permanently changed—it all still lingered. But for the first time, I saw a path forward. If I focused on excelling academically, if I pushed myself to do my best, I could carve out a place for myself in this new world. It wouldn't be easy, but I realized that learning and achievement could be my anchors, no matter where I was.

Later that spring, when my father sat at the dining room table reviewing our first report cards from Alameda Elementary, he signed my card and then, picking up Mario's report card, praised him for his strong grades. I watched the pride in my father's face, the way his approval felt like a prize to be earned. Wanting to measure up, I peeked at my brother's report card after my father had signed both of our report cards.

Even though my brother was thriving socially—making friends both at school and in the neighborhood—I noticed something surprising. My grades were just as strong as his, if not better. Despite feeling like an outsider, despite struggling to find my footing in this unfamiliar world, I was excelling academically. But what struck me even more was something I hadn't fully realized before: my father valued and praised my brother's good grades.

Desperate for my father's love and approval, I saw academic excellence as my way forward—a path to earn his recognition, to carve out my own place. If good grades mattered to him, then I would make them *my* advantage. It didn't matter that I hadn't yet made friends or that our family no longer felt the same, but I *could* control how hard I worked. And in that moment, something inside me shifted.

It was a quiet but powerful revelation of clarity. Achievement wasn't just about school anymore—it was about proving my worth. I didn't have to be defined by where I sat in the classroom, the school I attended, the neighborhood I lived in, or even the discomfort of feeling like an outsider. Not even being a girl would set my limits. I could achieve as much as, or even more than, my brother and his friends. That realization ignited something deep within me. This wasn't just about competition—it was about proving, to myself and to the world, that I could excel on my own terms. That I *would* excel.

From that day forward, I set higher standards for myself than anyone else did. I didn't wait for others to tell me what I was capable of—I decided for myself.

Finding Girl Scouts

Alameda Elementary offered a world of new opportunities and after-school activities that hadn't existed at Bradley Elementary. One of the first things my brother Mario did was join the Boy Scouts, and as always, I felt the urge to outdo him. But it was never about wanting to be a boy—I was fiercely competitive, determined to prove that I could do anything he could, if not more.

While Mario's involvement in the Boy Scouts was encouraged and celebrated, the idea of me joining a similar group never crossed my parents' minds. It simply wasn't on my father's or my mother's radar. Growing up in a traditional Mexican household, my mother wasn't aware that the Girl Scouts existed or that it was even a possibility for me.

It wasn't until a classmate invited me to a Girl Scout troop meeting near my house that I even realized it was an option. I wasn't particularly excited at first, but my classmate was persistent, urging me to ask my mother for permission. To my surprise, my mother immediately agreed—not because she knew what Girl Scouts was, but because she was thrilled at the chance for me to make a new friend.

That simple invitation became a turning point in my life. From the moment I stepped into my first troop meeting, I felt an unexpected sense of belonging. It wasn't just about earning badges, crafts, or camping—it was about discovery, independence, and learning to push past my own limits. More than anything, Girl Scouts instilled in me the foundations of leadership, courage, confidence, and resilience—life skills that would shape not just my childhood, but my entire future.

How a Science Badge and Library Card Led Me to NASA

One of my first Girl Scout outings was at an overnight campout at Apodaca Park in Las Cruces, New Mexico. After dinner and cleanup, I perched on a log, mesmerized as stars emerged one by one in the vast desert sky. A troop leader joined me, tracing patterns with her finger as she pointed out the Big and Little Dipper, the Milky Way, and bright individual stars and planets. Until that moment, I had only seen stars as scattered twinkling lights, never realizing they formed patterns with names and stories woven through history.

That overnight campout sparked something deep inside me—a fascination with the sky and the mysteries it held. Weeks later, during a troop meeting, we were selecting badges to earn. Without hesitation, I signed up for biking and camping. When my friends picked the cooking badge, I added my name to that list too. Then, my troop leader reminded me of my curiosity about the stars and encouraged me to earn a science badge. Inspired, I decided to take on a challenge I had never imagined before—building a model rocket to fulfill one of the badge's requirements. That moment wasn't just about earning a badge; it was the first step toward something far bigger than I could yet understand.

My early attempts were nothing short of disastrous. I had rockets that wouldn't launch, parts that broke, and failures that felt, at times, insurmountable. But with each failure came a lesson. My troop leader never let me give up, reminding me that setbacks weren't the end but part of the process. In Girl Scouts, failure wasn't a defeat—it was a *First Attempt In Learning*.

I kept at it, driven by curiosity and persistence. When my first rocket was beyond repair, I had to send away for another Estes model rocket kit, waiting impatiently for it to arrive. When it finally did, I carefully assembled it, triple-checking every step. But once again, it failed. Frustrated but determined, I tried again. And again. On my *sixth* attempt, I held my breath as I ignited the model rocket. This time, my rocket soared into the bright blue New Mexico sky.

As I watched it disappear into the blue, a realization hit me with the same force as that launch—I could do science, and I *loved* it.

Seeing Beyond the Visible

By fourth grade, we had settled into our home on Kay Lane and had grown familiar with more than just our immediate neighborhood—we also knew the path to the city's adobe public library by heart. My mother trusted my brother and me to go there on our own in the afternoons, allowing us to disappear into the world of books. Sometimes, I walked home alone because my brother was so absorbed in his reading that my mother had to call the library just to remind him to leave.

One afternoon, my curiosity pulled me beyond the two rooms filled with children's books and magazines. As I wandered deeper into the library, I entered its largest room—the section for newspapers and periodicals. There, spread across glossy magazine covers, was something that made me stop and stare. NASA astronauts in crisp white spacesuits, towering rockets poised for launch, and articles about IBM's latest space technology. The space race to the moon had captured the world's imagination, and in that moment, it captured mine.

I stood there, transfixed. The images of astronauts, engineers, and cutting-edge machines filled me with a sense of limitless possibility. They weren't just looking at the stars; they were *reaching* for them. They were solving problems, building machines, exploring the unknown. They were at the frontier of something bigger than themselves. The idea that humans could leave Earth, could break barriers that had stood for centuries, made me feel something I had never felt before—a deep, undeniable pull toward something greater.

No one on those covers looked like me, but that didn't stop me from imagining myself among them. If they had figured out how to get to space, I could figure out how to be part of their world. Determined to learn more, I devoured every article and book I could find about the space program. That's when I made an important discovery—if I wanted to be part of that world, I had to excel in math and science. The future I wanted wasn't built on idle dreams. It was built on knowledge, on skills, on mastery.

Even though there were no women in those pages, I didn't see that as a barrier. Instead, I saw a challenge. I realized something powerful: *I didn't need to see someone like me to believe I could be there—I just needed to see the possibility.* My success wouldn't come from waiting for an invitation or for someone to show me the way. It would come from the work I put in. The challenge wasn't about proving I belonged; it was about mastering the skills to get there. If I could do that, then belonging wouldn't be a question—it would be a fact.

The Language of Math

From that moment, I became relentless in my pursuit of math and science excellence. When my teachers assigned only the even-numbered math problems, I tackled both the odd and even ones, pushing myself beyond what was required. I wasn't just learning for a test—I was preparing for my future.

My dedication didn't go unnoticed. Two different elementary school teachers handed me the *math teacher's edition*, challenging me to push myself even further. They saw my hunger, my drive, and instead of holding me back, they gave me the tools to go further. I studied every equation, every formula, not just to understand them, but to *own* them. The more I practiced, the sharper I became, fueling a virtuous cycle where effort led to mastery, and mastery built confidence.

Math became more than just numbers on a page—it became *my* language, something I understood and wielded with certainty. Unlike other subjects, it wasn't open to interpretation. It had rules, structure, and a fairness that set it apart. In a world where so much felt uncertain or beyond my control, math was my constant, my equalizer. It was a level playing field where I could compete head-to-head with anyone. There were no opinions, no biases—just problems to solve and solutions to find.

It became more than a subject; it became a tool, a way to prove—to myself and to others—that I could rise to any challenge. That realization lit a fire inside me. If I could train my mind, if I could sharpen my skills, I *could* compete. I *would* compete.

Choosing to Compete

As I stood in the Thomas Branigan Library that day, I made a bold decision—I would learn the math and science required for those NASA and IBM roles, regardless of the fact that I didn't see any women in them. The absence of others who looked like me didn't discourage me—it *fueled* me.

I knew that if I focused on learning what was necessary, I could compete. And if I could compete, I could push myself to master the skills needed to succeed. Math and science had a structure, a logic that wasn't subjective—you either solved the problem, or you didn't. There was no opinion, just the certainty of right and wrong answers. That clarity gave me an advantage.

I realized that success wasn't about waiting for someone else to clear the path; it was about developing the expertise, discipline, and resilience to open the doors I wanted to walk through—on *my* terms.

The clarity of that realization completely reframed how I saw the world. Instead of fixating on obstacles, I focused on preparation. Instead of wondering if I belonged, I set out to *prove*—first to myself, then to everyone else—that I did.

Mastering the skills didn't just build competence; it fueled my confidence, reinforcing a cycle of growth and achievement. This belief became more than just motivation—it became the foundation of who I was and how I approached every challenge that followed.

From Dirt Roads to the Stars

I didn't fully appreciate it at the time, but that mindset—the unwavering belief that with hard work, *anything* was within reach—became one of my greatest assets. It carried me through every challenge that followed, serving as an anchor when things got difficult and a driving force when opportunities arose.

From that moment on, I didn't wait for permission to chase my dreams. I built the skills to make them a reality.

That clarity became a defining trait, shaping how I approached every challenge. I knew that before I could prove anything to the world, I had to convince myself. The expectations for a girl like me—growing up in a traditional household in a small desert town, far from any major city—were modest at best. Girls weren't encouraged to dream big, to push boundaries, or to imagine themselves in fields dominated by men. But I refused to accept those limitations. I held myself to a higher standard.

With every challenge I tackled, with every skill I mastered, my confidence grew. I didn't waste time dwelling on the fact that the astronauts and engineers I admired didn't look like me. That wasn't what mattered.

What mattered was learning what they knew, mastering the skills that would allow me to follow their path. I wasn't waiting for permission or for someone to tell me I belonged. I had already decided: *I belonged wherever I was willing to put in the work to be.*

The first step to achieving anything is believing that you can. Dare to dream boldly—see your future with clarity, not as a distant possibility, but as something real and within your reach. If you want change, start by changing how you see the world and your place in it.

Success isn't just about talent or opportunity—it starts with holding yourself to a higher standard, even when no one else does.

That belief carried me from dirt roads to the stars.

2 | Create Opportunity

The Power of Courage

Knowing I could compete with my brother and the boys in math and science changed me—it was the first time I understood I could achieve more than anyone expected of me. But one revelation alone wasn't enough to carry me from the desert to NASA or Stanford. Dreams burned brightly within me, but I had to learn how to turn them into reality. That's where this chapter begins—with the pivotal lesson that opportunities aren't given; they're created.

As I reflected on the Stanford researcher's question—how I went from being a girl with a knack for math and science to working at NASA and IBM—a memory came flooding back. It wasn't about equations or career planning; it was about cookies.

Step by Step

When I first joined Girl Scouts, I was eager to participate in every activity—camping trips, science projects, outings—but I quickly realized we couldn't afford it all. I was crushed. My troop leader, Mrs. Provine, saw my disappointment and said, "No problem—you'll sell cookies." Her confidence in me was unwavering, but I had no idea what selling cookies entailed.

She sat me down and explained something that would forever change my approach to life. "To create an opportunity for yourself," she said, "start with a goal. Break it down into smaller, manageable steps. Work hard on each step, and when you hit a wall, ask for help."

Belief alone isn't enough—it must spark action. She walked me through the math of how many boxes I'd need to sell to fund my activities. The number seemed insurmountable until she broke it down by weeks and days. Suddenly, the impossible became possible. I threw myself into the task, knocking on doors and pitching cookies with newfound purpose and was able to sell even more cookies than my original goal, enabling me to participate in the summer camp activities.

Avon Calling

This wasn't a lesson I saw in my own family. My parents worked tirelessly and yet we lived paycheck to paycheck. The weight of their obligations and responsibilities often left them feeling trapped, unable to envision a path toward greater opportunities. Yet, my mother refused to let those limitations dictate our future. Determined to supplement the family income and support Mario's and my educational aspirations, my mother began selling Avon beauty products to friends and family. Her unwavering resolve, resourcefulness, and quiet sacrifices were a testament to her deep belief in our potential and her determination to help turn our hopes and dreams into reality.

She was strict, holding us to high standards, but we never doubted her love—it was evident in every effort she made to give us a better future. Seeing her commitment reinforced what Mrs. Provine had taught me: *Opportunity isn't about waiting for something to change. It's about taking action, working toward a goal, and persevering in the face of obstacles.*

Deliberate Practice

What I didn't know then—but understand now—is that this approach has a name: deliberate practice. Elite athletes, top executives, and world-class professionals all succeed by applying this method. They stretch themselves just beyond their current limits, stepping into the narrow space where growth happens—not so far that it feels impossible, but far enough to learn and transform.

This lesson became my foundation. I learned that every big goal, no matter how daunting, becomes achievable when broken into steps. And when obstacles arise, as they always do, seeking help isn't a sign of weakness—it's a strategic move.

You can't grow by staying where you're comfortable. And you can't succeed by attempting jumps that feel out of reach. True progress happens step by step, fueled by a mindset that embraces challenge, risk, and learning.

Every step forward builds on the last, pushing you higher, making the next step possible. *Growth isn't about taking one giant leap—it's about daring to take the next one.* Progress may not always be linear, but it's always within reach if you're willing to adapt, push yourself, and keep going.

"You Can Go There"

Dreams are more than fleeting wishes; they're powerful forces that can shape your decisions and focus your energy. I learned this in fourth grade, sitting in my classroom at Alameda Elementary. My teacher, Mrs. Baldwin, brought her college-age son to talk about his experience of going to college in another state far away from our small desert town.

After his visit, she showed us a slideshow of universities. When an image of Stanford University appeared—its red-tiled rooftops, sprawling lawns, and green hills—I blurted out, "I want to go there!" I had no idea where Stanford was, but Mrs. Baldwin stopped the slideshow, walked over, and looked me in the eye. "You're a smart girl and you can go there," she said.

Her words turned my casual declaration into something real. That dream became my "north star," guiding every choice I made. I researched Stanford, learning it would take not just great grades but also extracurricular activities and preparation far beyond anything I'd considered. I began to see that dreams weren't just abstract—they were blueprints for action.

Mrs. Baldwin's belief in me and Mrs. Provine's lesson in creating opportunities didn't just shape my aspirations—they became the foundation for how I approached challenges and opportunities for the rest of my life. From the fourth grade, I had my heart set on going to Stanford. It became my "north star," and every decision I made—studying harder, joining extracurricular activities, and even saving money—was aligned with making that dream a reality.

Creating Financial Opportunity

I knew early on that my family couldn't afford to send me to California or cover the cost of college, so I focused on building a financial path to Stanford. I felt confident that with strong grades I could secure a scholarship, so I sought out seasonal jobs during the summers and holidays to avoid compromising my schoolwork. I became a city recreational league umpire, counted store inventory, babysat, and even collected aluminum cans for cash. Each dollar I earned went into high-interest CDs to grow my savings.

By the time I was in eleventh grade, I had saved several thousand dollars and felt confident that I was on my way to Stanford.

But life often presents challenges that test our resolve. That year, my maternal grandmother, Leonore Monge, unexpectedly passed away from flu complications while visiting two of her daughters, my aunts, in Los Angeles. The funeral expenses were beyond what my aunts or my parents could afford, and we were told that without a casket and proper burial, my grandmother would be placed in a nameless pauper's grave.

In that moment, my savings became a lifeline for my family. Without hesitation, I used the money I had painstakingly saved to pay for my grandmother's funeral. It was a deeply painful decision, but it reinforced a powerful lesson: the goals we work toward are important, but the bonds of family and the responsibility to care for those we love are even more profound.

A Positive New Plan

I knew my dream of attending Stanford as an undergraduate was no longer realistic. My hard-earned savings, which I had planned to use for my education, had gone toward something more important, which was helping my family in a time of need. Without that financial cushion, the idea of moving from the desert Southwest to Palo Alto for four years seemed impossible.

But just because I couldn't get to Stanford right away didn't mean I had to abandon my dreams of working at NASA or IBM. If the path I had envisioned was blocked, I would find another way forward.

One day at the library, I stumbled upon a college catalog that listed different degree programs based on a student's interests and talents. Curious, I filled out the questionnaire, eager to see where my skills in math, science, and problem-solving might lead. The results were eye-opening: industrial engineering was a perfect match. The field focused on systems, people, and processes, all areas that fascinated me—and, most importantly, it required strong math and science skills.

Excited, I scanned the list of top industrial engineering programs in the country. To my surprise, one of them was at New Mexico State University, the state school right in my backyard. Suddenly, the next step in my journey became clear.

Determined to learn more, I wrote letters to several of the top programs, introducing myself and expressing my interest in the field. But instead of encouragement, I received little to no response—just generic brochures or polite rejections. I could have let that discourage me, but I had learned early on that waiting for opportunity wasn't the way forward. If I wanted a chance, I had to create one.

Since New Mexico State University had a good program, I decided to take matters into my own hands. I skipped a morning of classes and went straight to the university's industrial engineering department to meet with the department head, Dr. Hicks. I had no appointment, no formal introduction—just a strong desire to pursue this path.

When I arrived, I was lucky that he had time to see me. I introduced myself and told him I was interested in the program. At first, he gave me a skeptical look. Engineering wasn't a field where many expected to see a girl. It hadn't occurred to me until that moment that I would have to prove I belonged before I even started.

Dr. Hicks asked if I had good grades in math and science. Instead of answering with words, I handed him a copy of my transcript. He studied it for a moment, then looked up and said, "You are certainly qualified."

That one sentence changed everything.

In an instant, his demeanor shifted from skeptical to supportive. He began telling me about the opportunities available through the program and, most importantly, he handed me several scholarship applications—including one for the prestigious Sandia National Labs scholarship, which would cover all college costs, including tuition, fees, and books.

I had walked in that morning with nothing but a dream. I walked out with a real path forward.

That meeting taught me something profound: sometimes, the doors don't open until you knock. If I had waited for permission, for someone to tell me I belonged in engineering, I might have missed my chance. Instead, by showing up, by proving that I was capable and determined, I created an opportunity that might never have come otherwise.

The Most Important Oil Change of My Life

I applied for every scholarship I could find—music, academic, and engineering. I played percussion well, had earned many honors, so I qualified for music scholarships, and my grades earned me academic scholarships as well. But despite my deep interest in engineering, those scholarships weren't coming through. As the months passed and graduation neared, I felt the pressure mounting.

Then, one spring morning during my senior year, the principal at Mayfield High called me over the intercom to come to his office. When I walked in, two men were waiting in a conference room—one a scientist, the other an engineer from Sandia Labs. They had received my application for the prestigious engineering scholarship, but there was one problem: they had never awarded it to a female before.

They wanted to make sure I was serious about engineering. This scholarship was highly competitive, and they didn't want to award it to someone who might change her mind, taking the opportunity away from another qualified student who would finish the program. Their questions started immediately. Did I know the quadratic formula? Could I explain specific math and science concepts? Then, one of them asked if I had ever done anything mechanical with my hands.

"I change the oil in our car," I replied.

One of the men raised an eyebrow, clearly skeptical. "Walk me through it," he said.

So, I did. Step by step, I walked them through the entire process—naming the tools, explaining how to safely lift the car to access the drain plug, drain the old oil, replace the filter, put the plug back in with a new gasket if necessary, and refill with oil to the proper level. I described every detail, down to checking for leaks and disposing of the used oil properly. When I finished, there was a pause. One of the men leaned back, nodded, and said, "Change for the sake of change is not progress. I guess I just needed to meet you and see for myself."

At the end of the hour, they looked at each other, then turned to me. "We're approving your scholarship."

It was official. I had just cleared another hurdle I never expected to face—proving I belonged before I even had the chance to begin.

As I walked out of the office, I felt relieved, but also unsettled. Until that moment, I had seen math and science as purely objective. There was a right answer, and if you solved the problem correctly, that was all that mattered. But this interview showed me something new—my path forward in engineering and science wouldn't just be about solving equations. It would be about proving I belonged.

That evening, I shared the news with my parents. As we totaled up all the scholarships I had received, my mother pointed out that with the Sandia Labs' scholarship, all my college expenses were covered. That meant I had to turn down the other scholarships so other students could use that money for school. It was not right to keep the other scholarship money.

I knew she was right. I had everything I needed to move forward. It was time to take the next step.

Urgency vs. Importance

Before starting at New Mexico State University, I set my sights on the next goal—earning a master's degree in engineering from Stanford. I knew getting there wouldn't be easy. It meant I had to fully commit to excelling academically, earning top grades, and distinguishing myself among my peers. I would also need to have work experience.

While I enjoyed extracurricular activities, including playing on the NMSU women's basketball team my freshman year, I soon realized my future wasn't on the court—it was in engineering. I made a pivotal decision to focus my energy on what would truly propel me forward. It wasn't just about passion; it was about aligning my talents with my long-term vision. I still played basketball and racquetball for fun, but I knew my path to success would be forged through engineering.

Each summer, I worked at Sandia Labs, gaining hands-on experience in different roles. I started as a field engineer, then became a materials specialist, later moved into laboratory research, and finally worked in human factors in transporting nuclear material. Every role taught me something new, exposing me to a world I had never experienced before. The internships were invaluable, giving me real-world applications of the theories I learned in class and reinforcing my confidence that I was on the right path.

One of the directors, Mr. Quigley, noticed my enthusiasm and took the time to share a piece of advice that would stay with me for life. One day, he pulled a small card from his pocket and showed me his handwritten list of six key tasks—things that weren't just urgent, but truly important. He explained that success wasn't about reacting to every crisis or demand placed on you. It was about focusing on the strategic tasks that truly mattered.

He told me, "People often sacrifice what they *should* do because they get caught up in the lack of planning by others. If you want to be effective, learn to separate what's urgent from what's important."

That lesson resonated deeply. From that day forward, I began making my own daily lists—not just of tasks that needed to be completed, but of the actions that would genuinely move me closer to my long-term goals. Mr. Quigley's simple yet powerful strategy became a habit that has guided my productivity and focus ever since.

The work experiences at Sandia Labs were more than just internships—they shaped my understanding of engineering, problem-solving, and professional excellence. They gave me the confidence that I could thrive in this field. When I graduated from college, the impact of those experiences became even clearer. Mr. Quigley and another one of my managers wrote heartfelt letters to my parents, sharing their appreciation for my work ethic, curiosity, and contributions.

Reading those letters, I realized that my time at Sandia Labs had been more than just an opportunity for me—it had been a testament to the values I had been raised with. These letters were recognition for my parents as much as they were for me.

"The Promise of You"

Yet, I still dreamt of Stanford. But as the days in my senior year dragged on in silence, doubt settled in. Maybe I had aimed too high. As the President of Tau Beta Pi, the engineering honor society, I had received job opportunities, all of them close to home. Maybe it was time to accept the reality. Then, one afternoon, an envelope arrived. It was slim. Too slim. My stomach tightened; I had seen enough rejection letters to recognize one. Still, I had to know. Bracing myself, I tore it open.

And then—shock. Disbelief gave way to exhilaration. I had been accepted to Stanford University. The dream I had first envisioned as a nine-year-old girl was no longer just a distant hope. It was real. It was happening.

The next morning, I rushed to the Engineering department, eager to share the news with the professors who had championed me. As I beamed with excitement, one of them asked, *"Stanford is a private university—does your letter mention funding?"* My breath caught. I hadn't even thought about that. Heart pounding, I pulled out the letter and scanned it again. Nothing about financial aid. My excitement dimmed as a new worry took its place—how was I going to pay for it?

What I didn't know was that, behind the scenes, someone else had been working to help students like me reach their potential. Dr. Howard Adams, the visionary founder of the GEM Program, had been relentlessly building pathways for graduate engineering students to attend top-tier universities. His program partnered with many of America's leading engineering institutions, but it had never reached New Mexico State University—so I had never even heard of it, let alone applied.

Then, out of the blue, my parents' home phone rang. Back then, there were no personal mobile devices, and the best way to reach me was through our family landline. My mother answered, took down a message, and handed me a note when I got home.

"You need to call a Dr. Howard Adams," she said, her voice laced with curiosity. She had written down his number and added, "He said you can call collect."

Long-distance calls weren't cheap, so that offer stood out. I had no idea who Dr. Adams was or what he wanted, but something told me this call mattered. As I picked up the receiver to make the call, my pulse quickened.

The voice on the other end wasted no time. "Congratulations," Dr. Adams said. "Your Stanford education is fully paid for."

I froze. The words didn't seem real. Paid for? How? I had never applied for a GEM Fellowship. I hadn't even heard of the program. Doubt flickered in my mind—was this a mistake? Sensing my hesitation, Dr. Adams explained.

When he first approached Stanford's Graduate Engineering Admissions Office about the GEM Program, they had not been very welcoming. "We don't lower our standards for anyone," the admissions officer had said.

Dr. Adams had simply handed them his card. "I'm not asking you to. I'm confident there will be students who qualify. Call me when that happens."

And then, one day, Dr. Adams's phone rang. "You were right," the Stanford admissions officer admitted. "We have a woman from NMSU who has been admitted to the graduate Industrial Engineering program."

That woman was me.

Dr. Adams didn't hesitate. The moment he had the chance, he reached out to me, delivering the words that would change my life:

> **"Your Stanford education is fully paid for."**

I was stunned. The weight of years of effort, hope, and uncertainty came crashing down at once. "How did you know to do that?" I asked, still trying to grasp the reality of what he was telling me.

Dr. Adams' response was simple, yet profound:

> **"I didn't know you specifically. But I knew the promise of you."**

Those words struck deep. Someone I had never met had believed in me before he even knew my name. He had built a path, not just for me, but for students like me—those with talent, drive, and ambition who simply needed a door to open, a chance to step into opportunities they hadn't even known existed.

The GEM Fellowship was more than just financial support; it was freedom. It allowed me to step into Stanford fully focused on my engineering studies, without the shadow of financial strain or debt. But beyond that, it was a powerful reminder that success isn't just about hard work and vision—it's also about those who see potential in others and take action to make opportunities possible.

That day, I made a quiet promise to myself: *One day, I'll do the same for someone else.*

The team at the GEM Program didn't just fund my education—they believed in my potential. When they learned about my passion for space, they took it a step further, opening a door I never imagined: a job at NASA.

Eager to Go, but Torn to Leave

After a wonderful education and experience at NMSU, I graduated to face one of the hardest moments of my life. I packed my bags, leaving behind the world I knew best—southern New Mexico, my family, the comfort of familiarity. Saying goodbye at the El Paso Airport was gut-wrenching. As I hugged my parents and my sister Laura and brother Armando, I felt the weight of the moment—excitement and fear tangled together.

But the dreams I had been chasing since childhood gave me the courage to step forward. This was the path I had worked for, the future I had envisioned. It didn't make leaving any easier, but it made it necessary. Some dreams require sacrifice, and this was mine.

Hello NASA

I found myself at NASA's Jet Propulsion Laboratory, working on the historic Voyager 2 mission. It was more than a dream job—it was a front-row seat to discovery. I analyzed the telemetry data from Jupiter's moons, Io and Europa. I watched in awe as some of the first images of Jupiter's Great Red Spot arrived, a swirling storm larger than Earth, alive with movement and color. I wasn't just studying space; I was part of a mission rewriting humanity's understanding of the universe.

But the greatest lesson I learned at NASA didn't come from data analysis or planetary exploration—it came from a conversation over lunch.

My second-level manager, a man who had been the first in his family to attend college and later earn a doctorate, recognized something in me. He saw my drive, but he also understood something deeper—I came from a world where people didn't often leave their hometowns to chase dreams that stretched beyond the horizon.

As we sat eating burgers, I shared my ambitions: attending Stanford, working at IBM, pushing the boundaries of what I could achieve. He listened carefully, then leaned in with advice that was deceptively simple yet transformative: "Don't just set your goals—see them in your mind as if they've already happened."

He spoke from experience. When he set out to earn his PhD in astrophysics and land a role at NASA, there was no roadmap, no one in his family who had gone to college, no step-by-step guide to follow. It was uncharted territory. "You have to chart your own course," he said.

Then, he told me a story that stuck with me.

On his first day of graduate school, a professor warned the class that only a handful of them would make it to graduation. Instead of feeling intimidated, he made a decision—he would be one of those few. To cement that belief, he imagined the moment he would cross the finish line. He pictured himself at his doctoral hooding ceremony, standing tall in his academic regalia, shaking hands with faculty, stepping into NASA as an astrophysicist. That image became his north star, pulling him forward through the grueling coursework, the long nights, the inevitable setbacks.

But visualization alone wasn't enough. He didn't just dream—he sought out those who had already achieved what he aspired to do. He asked them how they made it, what obstacles they faced, and what strategies kept them on track. Their insights turned his vision into something more than a hope—it became a roadmap, a plan built on real experiences and proven steps. That mental image of his future wasn't just a wish; it was a foundation for action.

His words reshaped how I saw my own ambitions. Dreams weren't distant, unreachable things; they were destinations, and like any journey, they required a strategy, persistence, and deliberate action. It wasn't enough to want something—I had to see myself there, believe it, and take the steps to make it real.

Inspired by his story, I began to do the same. I didn't just dream about Stanford—I *saw* myself there. I pictured myself walking through its sunlit campus, surrounded by the red-tiled rooftops and palm trees. I imagined stepping into Silicon Valley, working at the cutting edge of technology, building the future rather than just dreaming about it. The more I immersed myself in the details, the more real it became. What once felt like a distant aspiration transformed into something tangible, something within reach.

That lunch wasn't just a meal; it was a turning point. My manager likely understood better than I did just how ambitious my goals were. He knew that, coming from my background, I was breaking new ground. But he also knew something else—if I could clearly visualize the full picture, not just the dream but the steps to get there, I could turn the improbable into reality.

He was right. That mental image became my anchor, giving me clarity and focus even when the odds were long and the path ahead felt impossibly steep. It wasn't just motivation—it was my strategy, a reminder that success isn't about waiting for the right opportunity. It's about seeing where you want to go and building the road to get there, one step at a time.

I wasn't just chasing dreams anymore—I was engineering them, building them with intention, one step at a time.

As Voyager 2 completed its flyby of Jupiter, capturing its final breathtaking images before slingshotting toward Saturn, I found myself at a crossroads. While the spacecraft embarked on its years-long journey deeper into the cosmos to go by Saturn, I was reassigned to the Solar Polar and Solar Probe mission. But this project would take decades—the materials and technology to survive the Sun's extreme environment had yet to be invented. My path, however, wasn't on hold. I wasn't waiting decades. It was time for my next move.

I had been admitted to Stanford University, and it was time to leave Southern California for Northern California. But I wasn't just bringing my NASA experience—I was carrying a mindset shaped by every challenge and breakthrough: *see the future you want and take deliberate steps to make it real.*

Stanford was the dream I had first envisioned at nine years old. Now, it wasn't just a dream—it was happening.

Saving Face

Stanford was a revelation. The graduate engineering program was a crucible of innovation, attracting the brightest minds from around the world. In the 1980s, my classmates weren't just students; they were trailblazers, many handpicked by their governments with a singular mission—to push the boundaries of semiconductors, personal computing, and software and to bring the future of technology back to their home countries.

The stakes were high. For many, excelling at Stanford wasn't just about personal achievement—it was about "saving face" for their families, their institutions, and even their nations. Every assignment, every exam carried the weight of expectation, not just for themselves but for those who had placed their trust in them. The competition was relentless. It wasn't enough to do well—you had to stand out, to prove your worth on a global stage.

Yet, despite the intensity, the energy was electric. The professors weren't just experts—they were the authors of the Operations Research textbooks I had studied at NMSU. The ideas being taught weren't just theoretical; they were shaping industries in real time. Stanford wasn't just about learning—it was about stepping into the future as it was being created.

Outside the rigorous engineering curriculum, I met students who were also taking classes at the Stanford Business School, preparing not just for technical careers, but for leadership roles that would shape entire industries. Their bold thinking intrigued me. Wanting to expand my perspective, I enrolled in a few business courses—and what I discovered surprised me. The analytical skills I had in science and engineering weren't just for solving technical problems; they were just as powerful in business strategy, decision-making, and leadership.

Stanford wasn't just an academic challenge; it was a transformation. It rewired how I thought about innovation, leadership, and impact. It wasn't enough to build technology—I wanted to drive it forward, shape industries, and lead teams capable of turning bold ideas into reality. Surrounded by classmates who were designing the future, I was ready to carve my own path.

Graduating from Stanford was more than just a milestone—it was a moment of immense pride for me and my family. My father, who had once questioned my ambitions, now had a favorite coffee mug that read "Proud Stanford Dad." It was a symbol, and it spoke volumes about how far we had come, both in my journey and in our relationship.

Collision with Reality

Like my classmates, I was ready to take on the fast-paced world of Silicon Valley. The only question was—where would I begin?

Despite my experience at NASA and Stanford, reality hit hard. Job fair after job fair, resume after resume—I kept coming up empty. In one of the few interviews I landed, the hiring manager looked at me and bluntly said, "You don't fit the image of a Silicon Valley engineer and what we are looking for on our team."

That moment stung. I had spent years proving my abilities in math, science, and engineering, yet here I was, being judged not by my skills but by expectations I had no control over. I had hit a wall.

At an impasse, I turned to a lesson I had learned as a Girl Scout: when stuck, ask for help. Beyond career fairs and job boards, I started reaching out to everyone I knew, asking if they had heard of any openings for engineers. That's when I learned about a facilities position at IBM in South San Jose. It wasn't the cutting-edge tech role I had dreamed of—it wasn't even close. But it was a way in.

So, I took it.

My first professional assignment after working at NASA? Designing the office furniture layout for the engineers who were designing the technology products. It was not what I had envisioned. But it was also my first step—a small one, but a step nonetheless—into a world that would ultimately redefine my career.

Moving Beyond Convention

I was grateful for the job at IBM, but I couldn't ignore the sting of watching my classmates land coveted roles at the hottest tech companies—Hewlett Packard, Intel, Apple, Tandem Computers. They were diving headfirst into the future of technology while I was managing office layouts. It wasn't exactly the start I had imagined for my career.

But I knew one thing: a foot in the door was still a way in. And just as I had once asked for extra homework to sharpen my math skills, I made it my mission to raise my hand for every extra task.

One day, my boss handed me what he called a "small job"—expanding the manufacturing floor space for a critical part of our plant's main product: large mainframe data storage devices. Everyone else was busy, and all I had to do was adjust the layout. He emphasized its simplicity. I saw something else—an opportunity.

I completed the assigned layout but didn't stop there. I started spending my lunch breaks talking to the first- and second-shift production line workers, bringing sandwiches and asking for their insights. What slowed them down? What bottlenecks frustrated them? What would make their jobs easier? Their feedback was invaluable.

Using their input, I designed an alternative layout that optimized workflow and improved efficiency. When it came time for the manufacturing meeting, I presented both designs: the conventional one my boss had asked for and the redesigned version based on the workers' input.

The head of manufacturing, Mike Hall, studied both plans. "We've always done it this way," he said, looking at the original design. Then he turned to the alternative. After a long pause, he nodded. "Let's try this approach—it's innovative."

Because demand for our products was skyrocketing, the new layout was implemented almost immediately. The results were undeniable—production efficiency surged, and output increased. Others were quick to take credit, even though they had originally scoffed at the innovative design.

Then, something unexpected happened—IBM announced they were building a new production facility at the San Jose Plant.

When it came time to select the lead facilities engineer for the new line, Mike Hall didn't choose the most senior person. He chose me.

What I didn't realize at the time was just how ambitious this new facility would be. IBM wasn't just building another building—it was creating a cutting-edge, state-of-the-art manufacturing facility designed to push the boundaries of innovation. The scale and urgency were unlike anything I had seen before. Construction moved at an intense pace, running seven days a week to bring the vision to life as quickly as possible.

And now, I had the opportunity to be part of something far bigger than I had ever imagined.

That moment was monumental to me. It was proof that opportunity wasn't about waiting for the perfect job—it was about taking what was in front of me and making it count.

That experience didn't just accelerate my career—it fundamentally reshaped how I approached leadership. I had always believed in the power of hard work, but I learned that hard work alone isn't enough. Real opportunity comes from going beyond expectations, questioning the status quo, and redefining what is possible. The people who truly make an impact don't just meet the standard—they set it.

I realized that success isn't just about executing tasks well; it's about taking control of the narrative. It's about recognizing where change is needed, seizing the moment, and bringing a perspective that challenges assumptions. When you do that, you don't just fit into the system—you reshape it. You establish the benchmark instead of following it.

By presenting both the conventional approach and a bold, more efficient alternative, I wasn't just completing an assignment—I was proving something bigger. My message was clear: "I understand how things are done here, and I also see a better way."

That ability—to honor the existing framework while offering fresh, valuable innovation—became a defining strategy for me. It not only earned the trust of leadership but positioned me as someone who could navigate tradition while driving transformation. It taught me that leadership isn't just about excelling in your role; it's about seeing what others overlook, having the courage to offer something new, and demonstrating the value of thinking differently.

From Concept to Reality

As I stood at the forefront of IBM's groundbreaking ceremony of the new manufacturing facility, I realized this was more than a career milestone. It was a moment of transformation.

Each step of my journey—from Girl Scout cookie sales to NASA and IBM—taught me that dreams alone aren't enough. Creating opportunity requires deliberate action, a willingness to ask for help, and an unshakable belief in your ability to succeed.

As I stood watching IBM's C-suite executives tour the facility where I had led the design of the manufacturing layout, I realized I wasn't just chasing dreams anymore—I was building a future where I could lead innovation.

This wasn't just about constructing a facility—it was about laying the foundation for a future filled with possibility. It was a testament to the truth that the path forward is never handed to you; it's forged with vision, determination, and relentless action. The harder you work, the more opportunities you uncover—opportunities that don't simply appear but are earned through persistence and purpose.

Opportunity doesn't arrive on its own. It's something you create—brick by brick, step by step—until what once seemed impossible transforms into something undeniable and inevitable. Each courageous step, each choice, builds momentum, turning dreams into realities and ambition into achievement.

3 | The Three Nos

The Power of Conviction

As I looked toward this new career vision for myself, I thought back to the lessons that had shaped me from a young age—the importance of making decisions, setting clear goals, and putting in the work to create opportunity. But there was another lesson from my early years that was absolutely invaluable as I ventured into realms where few, if any, looked like me: how to persevere through rejection. Goals are powerful, but reaching them requires conviction and resilience, especially in the face of "no."

The lesson began when I was a young Girl Scout selling cookies. Raised in a close-knit, Spanish-speaking community centered around our church, I wasn't naturally comfortable speaking to strangers. Selling cookies felt intimidating and uncomfortable. When I confided in my troop leader, she offered advice that became a personal mantra: *"Never walk away from a sale until you've heard 'no' three times."*

At first, this was a practical sales tip—find common ground, handle objections, and persist with confidence. That is easy to say, but in reality, it can be hard to do. That rule taught me not to see "no" as the end of the road, but as a challenge to reframe, reimagine, and push forward. Practicing it repeatedly taught me to lean in when I heard a no, instead of moving away. It became a pillar of my resilience, shaping how I approached everything from school to my career. But over time, it became much more.

The First No: "Girls Like You Don't Go to College"

One of the earliest tests of this lesson came in high school. Sitting in the waiting area for a session with the college counselor, I was met with skepticism before I even walked into her office. She looked at me and declared, "Girls like you don't go to college."

By that time, I had been practicing the rule of the three nos for years. Instead of feeling the sting of rejection, I recognized it immediately as the "first no." I calmly walked into her office, and sat down. When she asked what I wanted to study, I replied confidently, "I want to be an engineer." She laughed dismissively: *"Girls aren't engineers!"* That was the "second no." But I didn't falter. I asked for the information I needed and left her office, determined to prove her wrong.

I pursued my dream of becoming an engineer, starting at NMSU and ultimately breaking barriers as one of the first Hispanics to earn a master's degree in engineering from Stanford. Becoming an engineer led to a milestone that felt almost surreal: my first job as a rocket scientist at NASA's Jet Propulsion Labs. But this achievement was more than a response to those who underestimated me—it was a testament to the power of perseverance, a refusal to let the doubts of others define my potential, and a commitment to reaching heights no one thought possible. My journey was proof that when you hold fast to your vision and rise above limitations, you can transform even the boldest aspirations into reality.

The Second No: "You Don't Fit the Mold"

Years later, in the 1980s, at IBM—the very company that had captivated my imagination as a child and represented my first corporate dream job—I encountered yet another series of resounding "Nos." IBM wasn't just a job; it was the pinnacle of technological innovation at the time, the largest and most powerful technology company in the world. And yet, even here, in the place I had once idealized, I found myself standing at the crossroads of rejection and perseverance.

Fresh off the success of leading a state-of-the-art manufacturing facility project, I witnessed firsthand how top executives toured the site, pausing to admire the innovations I had introduced. My designs not only improved productivity and efficiency for workers but also reimagined the manufacturing floor—structured so that executives could visually inspect operations without donning cleanroom suits. It was a moment of validation for my innovative designs.

Inspired, I set my sights higher. I asked my manager what it would take to climb IBM's executive ranks. His response? Dismissive laughter—loud, unmistakable.

Undeterred, I reframed my question with quiet determination: "If someone from the plant were to become a top IBM executive, what skills or experiences would they need?"

My manager barely hesitated before rattling off a list: "First, you have to carry a bag." Seeing my confusion, he rolled his eyes and clarified—it was industry jargon for being a sales rep. Then, without pausing, he continued, "You'll need experience in product management, international roles, enterprise marketing, and running a P&L."

At the time, I had no idea what "P&L" (profit and loss) meant. I could have asked, but I already knew how my question would be received—another dismissive look, another reminder of how much I *didn't* know. So instead, I kept quiet and made a mental note. His list wasn't just words to me; it was a blueprint. A challenge. A roadmap I hadn't known I needed.

That moment became a turning point. I didn't just absorb what he said; I turned it into a personal mission. Each requirement he listed became a rung on a ladder I was determined to climb. I wasn't waiting for permission, for validation, or for someone to hand me the next opportunity. If these were the skills I needed to rise, then I would find a way to master them, one by one.

This approach became a defining strategy in my career. Even when the path ahead wasn't clear, I trained myself to look beyond the uncertainty and break my ambitions into tangible steps. When I didn't know the rules, I asked. When I sensed barriers, I looked for ways around them. I learned to listen for the unspoken expectations—the experiences no one explicitly told you were necessary but were quietly required for advancement.

Where others saw limitations, I saw a puzzle to solve. When someone dismissed me, I didn't argue—I adapted. Every skill I gained, every experience I sought out, was another brick in the foundation of a career I was intentionally building. I wasn't just checking boxes; I was constructing something bigger, proving—first to myself, then to others—that ambitious goals aren't achieved by waiting. They are built through focus, persistence, and the willingness to chase knowledge, no matter where it leads.

Because, in the end, success isn't about knowing everything from the start. It's about being willing to learn, to push forward, and to see every challenge not as a roadblock—but as a door waiting to be unlocked.

First Step: Carry a Bag

I had my checklist, and first up was sales. IBM's prestigious Sales Training Program was legendary—considered the gold standard in the industry. At the time, IBM wasn't just another tech company; it was *the* technology company, setting the pace for innovation and business transformation. This training program was more than just a learning opportunity—it was a launchpad for high-impact roles, a proving ground for the best and brightest. For someone like me, with a technical background and a hunger to advance, it was the perfect next step.

Silicon Valley was booming, and IBM needed sales reps who could do more than just pitch a product. They needed people who could translate complex technology into real-world business solutions—who could sit across from a client, listen to their challenges, and connect the dots between their problems and IBM's cutting-edge offerings. It was exactly the kind of strategic thinking I thrived on. I knew I could do this. I was ready.

Or so I thought.

What started as excitement quickly turned to frustration. Rejections piled up, each one a fresh sting, each one a blow to my confidence. Not the right fit. Not enough experience. We're looking for something different. The words varied, but the message was the same: No.

It would have been easy to take the hint, to accept that this door simply wasn't going to open. But I wasn't wired that way. If the front door was locked, I wasn't going to stand outside and wait—I was going to find a side door, a window, a crack in the foundation—anything that would get me through.

I refused to let rejection define my limits. If the traditional path was closed to me, I would create my own.

I started by studying the people who had made it into IBM's elite Sales Training Program. Who were they? What did they have that I didn't? Where had they worked? What skills had they mastered? I dissected their

The Three Nos

career trajectories like a puzzle, searching for the missing piece that would unlock my own entry. Slowly, a strategy took shape—an unconventional, backdoor approach that would make it impossible for IBM to overlook me.

That's when I reached out to George, an "old-school" IBMer with decades of domestic and international sales experience. He was a fixture in the company, the kind of person who knew everyone and everything about IBM's culture.

We met for tea one afternoon, and from the moment he started talking, I knew this conversation was a goldmine. He regaled me with stories from his long career—deals that had been sealed in boardrooms, partnerships solidified over late-night negotiations, and breakthroughs made not just with brilliant pitches, but with the right words, at the right time, in the right room.

Through his stories, I began to understand that IBM's sales culture wasn't just about selling a product—it was about relationships, trust, and knowing how to navigate the unspoken rules of business. It was about anticipating client needs before they were even voiced. It was about confidence, presence, and understanding that sometimes, the real negotiation happened outside of the office, over dinner, or during a casual conversation between meetings.

Listening to George, I realized that getting into IBM sales wasn't just about proving I could do the job—it was about proving I could be the kind of person IBM wanted in the role. It wasn't just about mastering the sales process; it was about understanding the mindset, the culture, and the unspoken rules that set top performers apart.

Finally, I leaned in and asked the question that had brought me there: "What does it take to get into sales?"

George didn't hesitate. He rattled off a list of qualifications—experience with high-value clients, strong communication skills, a track record of problem-solving. I nodded along, taking mental notes. But then, he paused, studied me for a moment, and hit me with something I hadn't expected:

"It's not just about your skills. Sometimes, it comes down to being *pleasantly persistent, likable,* and *looking the part* of an IBM rep." His words struck me like a lightning bolt. Up until that moment, I had believed that success was built solely on expertise, hard work, and results. But George was telling me something different—something I hadn't considered in such stark terms. *It wasn't just about what I knew. It was about how I carried myself, how I built relationships, how I positioned myself for the opportunities I wanted.*

At first, his words felt almost unfair. Shouldn't my skills and drive be enough? But the more I thought about it, the more it made sense. Business—especially at a company like IBM—wasn't just about what you could do on paper. It was about *who* wanted to work with you, *who* saw potential in you, and *who* was willing to open doors for you.

For someone who had spent years in the technical trenches, solving problems behind the scenes, this was a revelation. *Mastering the work wasn't enough—I had to master the game.*

That meant I had to refine how I presented myself—not just my resume, but my presence. I had to ensure I was top-of-mind for the right people, not just as a capable candidate, but as someone they *wanted* to see in the role. I needed to make my ambitions clear, be intentional about building relationships, and project the confidence and polish of someone who already belonged in the Sales Training Program.

This wasn't about changing who I was. It was about strategically showcasing what I already had—making sure my drive, intelligence, and potential weren't just noticed but *remembered.*

George had given me more than advice—he had given me the key to shifting my approach. I walked away from that conversation with a new understanding: the door to IBM sales wouldn't open because of my skills alone. I had to knock on it, *again and again*, until the right people *wanted* to open it for me.

From that day forward, I committed to dressing for the role I aspired to next, ensuring my appearance aligned with the professional image I wanted to project. Unsure of what "looking the part" meant as a woman in a world where female executives were still rare, I sought guidance. I hired an image consultant, forming a lifelong friendship that taught me how to navigate this uncharted territory. Together, we crafted a professional look that balanced authority with authenticity—a critical step in defining my presence as a leader.

George's advice became a cornerstone of my career: success isn't just about mastering the written rules—it's about understanding the *unwritten* ones. I realized that technical expertise alone wouldn't open doors. Soft skills—confidence, communication, and projecting a sense of belonging—were just as critical. This insight transformed how I approached my goals. Breaking through wasn't just about ability; it was about *owning the room*, carrying myself with purpose, and proving—through every interaction, every detail—that I was ready for the next level.

With that shift in mindset, I attacked the challenge with renewed focus—and an updated wardrobe. For nearly a year, I watched job postings like a hawk, reapplying each time IBM sought engineers for their Sales Training Program. I paid close attention to "looking the part"—not just in my attire, but in my demeanor. I studied how successful IBM reps walked, talked, and commanded attention. They had a presence—an unshakable belief that they *belonged*. If I wanted that seat at the table, I needed to project that same level of confidence.

Month after month, the rejections kept coming. And with each rejection, the sting was real. But quitting was never an option. Every rejection was just another push to refine my approach. Throughout it all, I stayed in touch with George, keeping him updated on my progress—or lack thereof. At times, the waiting, the uncertainty, the *not knowing* whether my persistence would ever pay off gnawed at me.

After almost a full year of relentless pursuit, doubt started creeping in. Had I been chasing something that simply wasn't meant to be? Maybe I should set my sights elsewhere, take a different path. But before I could entertain that thought for too long, I decided to reach out to George one more time.

This time, his response caught me off guard.

"I've been waiting for your call," he said. "IBM has a spot for you in their Sales Training Program."

For a moment, I just sat there, letting his words sink in. Relief, excitement, and validation all flooded in at once. I had *done it*.

But curiosity lingered. "Would you have reached out to me if I hadn't called?" I asked.

On the other end of the line, I could *hear* his smile. "I knew you'd be persistent enough to follow up," he said. "That's exactly why I was counting on you to take the initiative."

And in that moment, it hit me—persistence wasn't just about perseverance. It was about *demonstrating* my drive, my commitment, my readiness to seize an opportunity the moment it presented itself. It was about proving—not just to IBM, but to *myself*—that I was someone who would *not* be ignored.

That moment wasn't just a win; it was a powerful validation of everything I had learned. A year of relentless effort had finally paid off, and the door I had been knocking on so insistently was now wide open. But more importantly, I had cemented a truth that would guide me for the rest of my career: *persistence, when paired with preparation and adaptability, can transform even the most elusive opportunities into reality.*

Success isn't just about talent. It's about *staying resolute* when doors don't open on the first knock. It's about pushing forward when the path isn't clear, trusting in the work you've put in, and having the courage to make that one extra call, send that one extra email, show up *one more time*—because that might be the moment that changes everything.

Taking a Leap

My experience in IBM sales was nothing short of exhilarating. I learned that when I faced a "no" in a sales conversation, instead of trying to change the customer's mind, I focused on how I could help them achieve better outcomes. As a result, I earned a coveted spot in the 100% Club, a recognition reserved for top performers and even had the privilege of taking clients on the IBM corporate jet—a heady experience for a young professional carving out her place in the tech world. Each deal, each challenge, honed my skills and deepened my understanding of the fast-evolving industry.

Working as an IBMer was both professionally enriching and personally meaningful. The company not only provided me with the tools to excel but also stood by me during a personal tragedy, offering a level of support that left a lasting impact. Over the years, I thrived in the fast-paced sales environment, mastering the art of relationship-building and navigating the complexities of the tech industry.

Yet, as rewarding as the experience was, I began to feel the pull toward something new. I had honed my skills, achieved significant milestones, and now found myself ready for the next challenge. One day, a colleague mentioned in passing that he was leaving IBM to join Apple—a daring, unconventional tech company that was redefining the industry. Apple's innovative spirit and bold approach intrigued me, but at the time, it was just a passing conversation.

Not long after, that same colleague reached out with an unexpected offer: a role at Apple in product channel marketing for the domestic market. It wasn't just an opportunity; it was a chance to step into the forefront of a company that was reshaping the future of technology. It felt like a calling to take the leap and embrace a new chapter and check off the next item on my checklist.

The Third No: "You're Not Qualified"

Working at Apple was a world apart from IBM—faster-paced, unconventional, and infused with a spirit of innovation that electrified every corner of the company. IBM was a technology giant; Apple was the bold disruptor, the archetype of the rebellious tech upstart. I threw myself into learning everything I could, channeling my analytical skills to support enterprise sales teams in landing major deals through distribution partners with global multinational customers.

One day, at an all-hands meeting, the new executive for Apple Pacific mentioned a strategic push for growth in the Latin American region. Intrigued, I scanned the job postings and found a position identical to my role in the United States but focused on Latin America. This was my chance for international experience, which was another item on my skills and experience professional checklist. Confident, I scheduled a meeting with HR, fully expecting to be a strong candidate since I was already doing the job domestically—and I spoke Spanish well enough to manage.

The recruiter barely glanced at my resume before saying, *"You're not qualified."* She explained that prior international experience was a strict, non-negotiable requirement. I countered every argument I could muster, but her answer was firm: no previous international experience, no job. That was my first "no."

Over the next six months, I spoke with everyone I could, from the hiring manager to members of the international team, but the answer was always the same.

Finally, I decided to try a different approach. Leveraging my analytical skills, I dove into Apple's sales data, identifying untapped revenue potential in the Apple Pacific region with signed global contracts with multinational accounts. This was in the era before the widespread use of CRM (Customer Relationship Management) software. I created a compelling presentation projecting millions of dollars in untapped revenue, complete with logos of global companies and country flags across the Apple Pacific region.

Then I thought, "Who would care about this presentation?" The gatekeepers clearly didn't. But the head of sales for Apple Pacific might. Timing my approach perfectly, I caught the VP of Sales by the elevators one morning. *"John,"* I said confidently, *"I can show you how to grow sales by millions of dollars next year with signed global contracts."* Intrigued, he invited me to a nearby team room and gave me five minutes to share my findings.

Flipping through the presentation, he nodded, his interest clearly piqued. "This is impressive," he said. "I had no idea we had so many multinationals with signed global contracts in the Apple Pacific region." As he stood, reaching for the presentation, I instinctively placed my hand on it, meeting his gaze with quiet determination. "It comes with me," I said firmly.

He paused, sizing me up, and then gave a slight nod. That moment felt like a silent agreement—an unspoken acknowledgment of my resolve. This approach became a defining hallmark of my professional growth as a trailblazer: persistence in the face of multiple "nos," taking the initiative to do the job before I had the job, dressing the part for the role I aspired to, and identifying and communicating with the key stakeholder who would benefit most from my strategy. In this case, I focused on the senior executive of sales as he was the one with the authority to approve my hiring and had the most to gain from the value I proposed to bring. It was a calculated yet determined approach, one that consistently turned ambition into opportunity.

True to his word, he made it happen. I got the job, stepping into a new role that offered not just a career milestone but an extraordinary opportunity: the mentorship of Hector Saldaña. Hector wasn't just a leader; he was a visionary who had built the Apple Latin American division from the ground up and later orchestrated the remarkable turnaround of Apple Japan, driving its sales beyond $1 billion in just a few years. His expertise, mentoring, and insight became a guiding force as I navigated the complexities of international markets and learned to think on a global scale.

Even as I forged new paths professionally, I recognized the invaluable role of mentors who had navigated their own uncharted journeys. Hector, my first mentor at the senior executive level, was instrumental in shaping my approach to leadership and strategy. He emphasized the power of a pragmatic, strategically focused operational plan to transform opportunities into sustainable business success. Through his mentorship, I developed a cross-functional, results-driven mindset and a disciplined approach to executing ambitious goals with clarity and precision.

This opportunity to work internationally was far more than a simple job transfer; it was a defining moment. I had discovered that breaking through walls often requires finding a way around them, rethinking strategies, and seizing opportunities in unexpected ways. This wasn't just a step forward—it was a leap into an entirely new realm of possibility.

"You Want Fries with That?"

One of Apple's greatest growth opportunities in Latin America was hidden in plain sight: peripheral products like printers, networking equipment, and software. While many dismissed this as a low-priority market—assuming most sales would flow to pirated products or through the United States—I saw a critical gap that could either constrain or catalyze Apple's growth in the region.

Without a strong distribution channel for these products, Apple's core business would face unnecessary friction. Customers needed more than just a computer—they needed the full ecosystem to maximize its value. It was the classic "Do you want fries with that?" moment. Just as fast-food restaurants increase sales by offering complementary items that enhance the main purchase, Apple had the opportunity to drive additional revenue while improving the customer experience. Without seamless access to the right peripherals, customers couldn't fully integrate Apple products into their workflow, leading to lost sales and lower adoption rates. Recognizing this, I identified a way to increase sales by strengthening Apple's approach to adjacent markets. Rather than viewing peripheral products as secondary, I saw them as a key opportunity to drive growth and enhance Apple's overall market presence.

The key was partnerships. I collaborated with a major distributor to utilize Apple's distribution network across the Pacific region, including Latin America. This network didn't just move peripheral products—it created an infrastructure that made add-on sales effortless for an Apple reseller. Customers needed more than just a computer—they needed the full ecosystem to maximize its value. Apple customers became more likely to purchase printers, software, and networking equipment when those products were conveniently available and well-integrated into their purchasing journey. This approach not only unlocked new revenue streams but also reinforced Apple's ecosystem, making it more attractive and complete.

In less than a year, what was once an overlooked market became a thriving $250 million revenue stream in third-party sales, strengthening Apple's position in the Apple Pacific region. More importantly, it reinforced a fundamental business principle: sustainable growth isn't just about selling more of the core product—it's about selling with a strategic approach. When customers have access to the right add-ons, they don't just spend more; they get a better, more complete experience with the product. This not only increases immediate revenue but also strengthens long-term customer loyalty. By making it easier for customers to fully integrate Apple's technology into their daily lives, we weren't just selling accessories—we were enhancing the overall value of Apple's ecosystem.

As part of this initiative, I was introduced to a networking company affiliated with Tandem Computers, which was struggling to boost its sales efforts in Latin America. This opportunity was a clear example of how thinking beyond immediate objectives and acting with intention could open unexpected doors for professional growth.

On paper, I was the ideal candidate for the role—I had the right experience, the necessary technical expertise, and a proven track record of driving sales in emerging markets. Yet, as the interview progressed, I noticed an underlying hesitation from the hiring manager. His questions were guarded, his responses measured. Something didn't add up.

I knew I had checked every box, yet there was a disconnect between my qualifications and his enthusiasm. Instead of ignoring the tension, I decided to confront it directly. "Is there something about my background or experience that concerns you?" I asked.

At first, he hesitated, but after a moment of silence, he spoke candidly. "To be frank, I don't feel safe traveling in Latin America myself, and I'm uncomfortable putting a female in that position."

His words were blunt, and his honesty surprised me. Instead of being discouraged, I saw an opportunity to address his unspoken doubts head-on. "Which country are you most concerned about?" I asked. "If I go there and meet with clients, will you give me the job?"

He studied me for a moment, clearly taken aback by my confidence, then nodded. "If you can do that, the job is yours."

Keeping my commitment, I traveled to the region and met with key clients. I proved my capability firsthand and secured the position in the process. But earning the job was just the beginning. Once in the role, I applied my strategy of presenting two well-crafted proposals—one conventional, the other forward-thinking—to drive major installations of cutting-edge fiber-optic networks. This approach led to successful deployments first in Venezuela and then at Mexico's Bolsa de Valores stock exchange. The results not only revitalized the company's business in the region but also positioned me as a leader who could navigate complex environments, break through barriers, and turn challenges into opportunities.

Persistence, Creativity, Courage, and Conviction

Whether it was selling cookies, securing a role in IBM sales, or breaking into Apple's international division, the lesson remained the same: obstacles aren't insurmountable. Each "no" is a challenge to find another way forward. The belief in yourself and your ability to learn, adapt, and grow is the foundation for turning setbacks into stepping stones.

The path to success is rarely a smooth, upward climb. It's more like a winding mountain trail—unpredictable, steep, and full of obstacles that test your endurance and resolve. There are moments when progress feels effortless, but just as often, you find yourself staring at what seems like an impossible wall, unsure of how to move forward.

And let's be honest—when someone looks you in the eye and tells you "no," not just once, but over and over again, it's more than just a professional setback. It feels personal. A gut punch that knocks the wind out of you.

The instinct to push back, to argue, to prove them wrong in the heat of the moment is almost reflexive.

But I had to learn—through trial, error, and sheer determination—that reacting emotionally wouldn't get me where I wanted to go. Instead, I had to channel that energy into something more powerful: persistence, strategy, and action. Success wasn't about proving someone wrong in the moment; it was about staying focused, moving forward, and finding a way around the barriers in my path. The real test wasn't whether I faced rejection, but how I responded to it.

Instead, I discovered the power of pausing. Taking a breath, silencing the instinct to push back, and focusing on what lay beneath the "no." I learned that rejection wasn't always about me—it could also be about the other person's fears, assumptions, or past experiences. My job wasn't to bulldoze through resistance, but to find the cracks in it—the moments of hesitation, the underlying concerns, the unspoken doubts—and use those as my entry point.

Finding common ground was often the key to unlocking doors that seemed permanently shut. Sometimes that meant connecting through shared interests—sports, travel, or even a mutual appreciation for a hobby. These seemingly small moments of rapport had the power to shift the dynamic, transforming a skeptical gatekeeper into a potential ally. What felt like an unmovable barrier just minutes earlier could suddenly become a conversation, a possibility, a path forward.

Every rejection taught me to approach with curiosity instead of frustration. To listen more than I spoke. To ask better questions. To resist the urge to take offense and instead dig deeper—what was really holding them back? What were they not saying? If I could understand the real reason behind the hesitation, I could address it directly and shift the conversation from resistance to possibility.

But this approach requires patience, and patience can be exhausting. Some people seem to take pleasure in making things harder than they need to be, wielding their authority with an unspoken "I'm up here, and you're down there" attitude. It's frustrating. It's humbling. And at times, it's deeply discouraging. There were moments when I wanted to walk away, when the weight of pushing forward felt heavier than the reward ahead. But I had a choice: let their resistance define my limits or find a way around it.

That's when I realized that perseverance alone isn't enough. Success isn't just about pushing through—it's about adapting, strategizing, and mastering the art of building bridges. Because in the end, the most powerful way to change someone's mind isn't through force—it's through connection.

Success isn't about avoiding the hard moments—it's about facing them head-on. It's about standing at the base of what feels like an impossible climb and taking that first step anyway.

It's about pushing forward even when doubt creeps in, even when rejection stings, even when you feel like you're walking alone. You acknowledge the struggle, the setbacks, and the frustration—but you don't let them define you. Because the true test isn't whether the path is difficult; it's whether you have the courage and the conviction to keep moving forward despite it.

Strength isn't in never failing—it's in showing up again and again, proving to yourself that the journey is worth it. Every obstacle, every unexpected twist, every moment of self-doubt isn't a reason to stop; it's part of the story that makes your success more meaningful. The hard-fought wins, the moments where you refused to back down, are the ones that shape you.

Dreams aren't handed to you. They're built—through resilience, through creativity, through the sheer conviction to keep going when others might quit. And if you're someone who is forging a new path, breaking barriers, or challenging the status quo, you'll hear "no" more times than you can count. It will come from people who can't see your vision, who underestimate you, who are too afraid to take risks themselves. But every "no" isn't the end—it's an opening. It forces you to rethink, to adapt, to push beyond what others see as limits. Each rejection sharpens your resolve and fuels your ability to innovate, making you not just stronger, but smarter and more capable.

If there's one thing I know for certain, it's this: success is never a straight line. It's a path filled with roadblocks, unexpected detours, and moments where the doubt—both yours and others'—feels overwhelming. But perseverance isn't just about pushing through obstacles, it's about learning from them. It's about turning every rejection into a new approach, every failure into a lesson, every setback into an opportunity to grow. The people who make it aren't the ones who never struggle—they're the ones who refuse to stop.

The real key to success isn't about avoiding "no." It's about having the mindset that says, I will find a way—no matter what. When you trust in your ability to navigate the challenges, you don't just overcome obstacles—you transform them into stepping stones. And with every step forward, you become stronger, wiser, and even more unstoppable.

4 | When Everything Shatters

IBM wasn't just a company—it was *the* company, the gold standard of technology and business innovation. The phrase "No one ever got fired for buying IBM" wasn't just a corporate cliché; it was a reflection of IBM's dominance, a reputation built on trust, excellence, and cutting-edge solutions. At the heart of that success was its rigorously trained sales and marketing force, honed through IBM's legendary training programs. Being part of that program wasn't just about learning sales—it was a masterclass in strategy, persuasion, and problem-solving at the highest levels.

At 28, my life felt like a carefully orchestrated symphony of reaching milestones. I had earned a coveted spot in IBM's 100% Club, was taking clients on the IBM corporate jet, closing high-stakes deals in semiconductor and technology sales, and learning to navigate the pulse of Silicon Valley. Living in Menlo Park and working in Palo Alto, I was surrounded by a dynamic community of friends and colleagues. My days were filled with professional and rewarding challenges, and my nights were rich with friendship and activities. I played in a local soccer league, enjoyed tennis and hiking with friends, hosted vibrant Cinco de Mayo and holiday parties, and relished the satisfaction of seeing so many of my early dreams come to life—NASA, Stanford, IBM. *I had done it.* And from where I stood, the future seemed limitless.

I was riding high—driven, ambitious, and certain that with enough effort, I could shape my destiny. I believed that success was something you built through persistence and strategy, that setbacks were simply problems waiting to be solved.

But life, as it often does, had other plans.

Just as I was reaching new heights, an unthinkable tragedy struck.

In a single moment, my world shattered. A loss so profound, so staggering, that it left me breathless. Grief, shock, and shame wove together into something unrecognizable, something I couldn't outrun or outthink. It wasn't just pain—it was a rupture, tearing through the fabric of my life and my family, leaving us fractured in ways we could barely comprehend.

There are moments that divide your life into *before* and *after*. This was mine.

And in the wake of it, I was left searching for meaning, for solid ground, for any way to piece together a life that suddenly felt like it no longer fit.

The Day Everything Changed

September 3, 1985. It was the Tuesday after Labor Day, and I was sitting at my desk in the IBM Palo Alto branch office, sifting through emails, trying to settle into the rhythm of the workweek. But something was off. A strange, suffocating heaviness pressed down on me—a sadness so thick and unshakable that it made every task feel impossible. It wasn't just a fleeting bad mood. This was different. It was a weight I couldn't name, a darkness I couldn't explain.

By midday, my mind was still clouded, my body restless. I couldn't focus, couldn't think straight. Needing a break, I grabbed some materials that needed to be delivered to a client in Santa Clara, hoping the drive would help clear my head. The sun was shining, the Bay Area sky a brilliant blue, but my unease didn't lift. If anything, it deepened.

On a whim, I detoured to a nearby park, a place I loved for its sweeping vistas stretching from Palo Alto to the San Francisco Bay. I stood there, inhaling the crisp air, hoping that the vastness of nature would dissolve this inexplicable sorrow. But instead of comfort, I felt something else—a deep, almost primordial sadness, an ache that felt as ancient as the earth itself.

I forced myself to push forward, finishing my errand and dropping off the client's materials at the front desk. But I couldn't shake the unease, and rather than return to the office, I found myself driving aimlessly, lost in the storm of emotions I didn't understand. In those days, there were no mobile phones, no laptops tethering me to work. I had been completely disconnected for hours, adrift in a world that suddenly felt wrong.

Eventually, I turned toward home. My friend Liz was visiting from Michigan for the long holiday weekend, and the thought of seeing a familiar face was the only thing that felt grounding. But as I climbed the stairs to my apartment, my stomach twisted. Liz was standing at the door, her posture rigid, her face pale. Her eyes, wide with worry, locked onto mine.

I stopped cold.

"Something terrible has happened," she said, her voice trembling. "You need to call your Aunt Angelica or your cousin Cathy in Las Cruces."

My heart pounded, my breath shallow.

Something was very, very wrong.

The Moment When Everything Changed

The fact that I was being told to call my aunt or my cousin—not my parents—told me everything.

That was the moment my world split in two: *before* and *after*.

A chill jolted through me, a visceral shock that made my stomach lurch. My body knew before my mind did. Whatever had happened, it was beyond comprehension. A deep, sickening dread coiled inside me as I reached for the phone, my fingers suddenly became foreign and unsteady. The air in the room thickened, pressing down on me, making every movement slow, heavy, unreal. My friend Liz stood by me, her face etched with concern.

My aunt's voice trembled as she answered. And in the beat of silence before she spoke, I knew. I didn't know how, but I knew. In some way, the universe had already whispered the truth to me, had already rearranged itself in a way that made sense of the unexplainable weight I had felt all day.

Then, the words came, each one a hammer blow to my chest.

"Both your parents are dead," she sobbed. "Your father . . . he . . . he killed your mother and then himself."

My mind shut down in an act of self-preservation, drowning in a numbness so complete that for a moment, I felt nothing at all. My body refused to register the magnitude of what I had just heard, as if denying it would make it untrue. But the words were still there, echoing, reverberating in the air around me.

Somehow, my mouth formed words. I heard my own voice, distant and detached, telling her I would come immediately. But I wasn't really there, incapable of responding to an unimaginable horror.

Liz, my friend—my anchor—moved with quiet urgency, stepping in where I couldn't. She arranged my flight, packed my suitcase, made the decisions I was incapable of making. I sat frozen, my hands limp in my lap, staring into space as my world disintegrated around me.

The flight passed in a haze, my body rooted in the seat while my mind floated in a reality too surreal to grasp. The steady hum of the engines, the quiet murmur of passengers, the rustle of in-flight magazines—life moved on around me, untouched by the catastrophe that had consumed mine. I stared at nothing, feeling untethered, unmoored. I was there, but I wasn't there, suspended in a limbo between what had been and what awaited me, trapped in the space between disbelief and unbearable truth.

A House Marked by Tragedy

Arriving in Las Cruces late that night, I instinctually made my way to our family home. What I saw stopped me in my tracks. Yellow police tape crisscrossed the house—my childhood home, now a crime scene. The sight was surreal, the contrast between the familiar and the horrific almost unbearable. The place where my family had lived, where memories were etched into every room, was now marked by yellow caution tape broadcasting our tragedy and loss for all to see.

At my Aunt Angelica's house, I found my younger sister, Laura, in the quiet, protective care of my aunt and her sons, my cousins Manaces and Josue. No one had the words to make sense of what had happened, but they didn't need to—grief hung between us, unspoken yet suffocating. We were all trying to steady ourselves in a world that had suddenly become unrecognizable.

My brother, Mario, was staying with my Aunt Alma and Uncle Sam, who had taken him in during the immediate aftermath. Each of us had been scattered, placed in different homes like pieces of a shattered picture, trying to find some semblance of stability in the chaos.

The next day, at my Aunt Alma and Uncle Sam's house, the raw edges of the tragedy began to take shape, each revelation landing like a fresh wound. I sat in the dining room, surrounded by family, the air was heavy, thick with an unbearable stillness, the kind that only comes when grief is so profound, so all-consuming, no one knew what to say because there was nothing to say.

Everything had changed, and we were left with only the jagged remnants of what once was.

My cousin Cathy, one of Aunt Alma's grown children, sat beside me. Her hands trembled as she spoke, her voice barely above a whisper, as if saying it too loudly would make it even more real. She had been the one to identify my mother's body at the morgue.

The words hit like a wrecking ball, I stared at her, my mind trying to process the unbearable image she now carried—the stark finality of it, the cold, clinical space where my mother, *my mother*, had been reduced to a lifeless form waiting to be claimed. The thought made my stomach turn.

Then, my uncle spoke, his voice heavy with grief and something else—hesitation, as if he was unsure how much more I could take. But there was no mercy in this kind of truth. There was no softening the blow.

"Your father had called the police after shooting your mother—before turning the gun on himself."

The room tilted.

For a moment, I felt weightless, as though I had been untethered from reality entirely. The walls, the floor, the presence of my family—all of it blurred as my mind recoiled, refusing to accept what I had just heard. A rage ran through me, deep and involuntary. My mother's life had been stolen, and my father—*my father*—had been the one to take it. And then, he had chosen to leave this world too, leaving behind nothing but devastation.

The fragile composure I had clung to shattered. I pressed my hands against my face, as if I could block out the horror, as if I could somehow turn back time and undo it all.

But there was no undoing. No waking up from this nightmare.

The silence in the room was suffocating, pressing down on us like an invisible force. No one moved. No one spoke. Grief had drained the air from the space, leaving behind only the sound of our own breathing—shallow, unsteady. Each of us was crushed under the weight of shock, lost in the same unbearable reality, yet somehow isolated in our own separate pain.

Finally, Uncle Sam broke through the quiet, his voice steady but strained. "You need to go to the police. Make funeral arrangements. Meet with a lawyer." The words landed heavily, reminders of the impossible tasks ahead, each one sharp and cruel.

I swallowed hard, forcing my thoughts into order. "What about the house?" I asked, already dreading the answer.

Uncle Sam's face darkened. He shook his head, his voice low, almost a warning. "Don't go back there. It's still a mess."

The weight of his words sank into my bones, cold and unshakable. I didn't need details—I already knew. I could see it in my mind, clear as if I were standing there. The remnants of violence, the echoes of final moments frozen in time. What had been left behind. What had been stained. What had been shattered beyond repair in what had been my childhood home.

Rage and grief crashed over me in waves, twisting together into something raw and consuming. I looked around at the faces of my family—my aunt and uncle, my cousin, my brother. Stunned. Frozen in the paralysis of trauma. I could see it so clearly now: no one else could bear this weight. We were all drowning in the same storm, but someone had to grab the wheel. Someone had to move.

Though my heart felt shattered, something inside me shifted. A quiet, unshakable resolve. I couldn't let this horror swallow us whole. If my mother's life had been stolen, then at the very least, I would honor her memory by making sure we didn't break completely.

Together, Mario and I went to the police station, a place that felt cold and impersonal in the face of something so deeply personal. The officers played for us a recording—a final remnant of the tragedy. It was my father's 911 call.

We listened.

His voice filled the small room, the last echoes of a life unraveling, of a choice that had ripped everything apart. It was chilling, haunting, a moment that stripped away any remaining denial. This was real. This had happened. And there was no undoing it.

When the officer asked what we wanted to do with my father's pistol, there was no hesitation.

"Destroy it," Mario said, his voice firm, final.

And just like that, a piece of the past was erased. But no matter how many things we burned, buried, or tore down, the pain, the loss, and the irreversible truth of what had happened would remain.

No Longer Home

The next step was returning to the house—a place now cloaked in the echoes of horror. I arranged for a cleaning service, but nothing could have prepared me for what I was about to see. The images are seared into my memory: rooms filled with silent, haunting reminders of violence, and the cold, clinical work of erasing it all. After the crew finished their work, I stepped outside, only to feel another gut punch. At the end of the driveway, a pool of pink water had gathered, tinted with faint, unmistakable traces of red. I stood there, frozen, realizing with a sickening clarity—this was my mother's blood, washed out into the street, lingering in that puddle. It's a sight that would haunt me, resurfacing in my mind for years to come.

My younger brother, Armando, was stationed in Germany with the Army, making his way back home as quickly as he could. But in those early days, before he arrived, it was just Mario and me—two stunned siblings navigating an unthinkable nightmare.

We did our best to hold each other up, but the weight of our grief was crushing. Some moments, we managed to function, to push through. Other times, it was too much. The trauma, the anger, the sheer enormity of what had happened would hit us like a tidal wave, and we'd break down, lost in the wreckage of our shattered world.

Yet even in the depths of grief, life was relentless. It didn't offer time to process, it didn't pause for sorrow.

Decisions had to be made. Arrangements finalized. Calls placed. Documents signed. The world didn't stop—not even for this.

And so, the weight of responsibility settled onto my shoulders, heavy and inescapable. It was this, more than anything, that kept me from drowning completely. The crushing need to *act*—to make sure my family didn't completely fall apart—became my anchor, pulling me back just enough to keep moving forward. I wasn't ready to face what had happened, but there was no choice.

So, step by step, through the numbness and the pain, I kept going. Because someone had to.

Facing the Unimaginable

In July, just a few months earlier, I had spent a week in Mexico with my mother, visiting relatives. During that trip, she confided in me that now that Armando had joined the Army, she was ready to divorce my father. Even though I had long known they were deeply unhappy, her words left me grappling with a storm of emotions. How would they split up? The thought of our already fragile family fracturing even further was overwhelming. My father had taken the news hard and had started seeing a therapist, a step that felt both surprising and hopeful.

And now, after their deaths, I couldn't stop replaying those conversations in my mind. I wished I had probed deeper, talked through the unspoken tensions, or even helped map out a path forward. My father had been abusive in the early years of their marriage, but when my mother prepared to leave him, he changed. Still, the shadows of those early years lingered. Could I have done something—anything—to prevent this tragedy? The weight of that question crushed me as I faced the unimaginable: managing two burials for my parents under the most horrific of circumstances.

Grief blurred my days, but one thought stood out above all: this wasn't how things were supposed to end. I wanted answers, clarity, and some way to make sense of a heartbreak that felt impossible to bear. Instead, I was left with silence, unanswered questions, and the heavy responsibility of laying them both to rest.

I made the decision to bury my parents in separate cemeteries—an act of defiance against my father who had stolen everything from us. The thought of them side by side, as if they had left this world together in peace, was something I would not accept. My fury at my father burned too hot, my heartbreak over my mother too deep.

We did hold a joint funeral, and as I stood before those gathered, I felt my mother's presence, urging me toward something I couldn't yet grasp—forgiveness. But I wasn't ready. *How could I forgive?* How could I make peace with something so horrific? The wound was too fresh, the betrayal too raw.

Burying my father was painful, but burying my mother—*that* was unbearable.

As her casket was lowered into the earth, something inside me shattered. I could no longer hold back the tidal wave of grief. Without thinking, without caring who was watching, I flung myself onto her casket, clutching it as if holding on tightly might somehow stop the inevitable, might somehow keep her with me just a little longer.

She wasn't just my mother. She was my foundation, my fiercest protector, my greatest champion. She had believed in me before anyone else ever had—cheered for me when no one else even knew there was something to cheer for. Every challenge I had faced, every dream I had dared to chase, she had been there, her unwavering faith in me a constant, steady force.

And now she was gone.

How could I move forward without her voice lifting me up? Without her love anchoring me? The emptiness was unbearable, the pain so deep it felt like my very soul had been torn in half.

A crushing sense of loss wrapped itself around me, consuming and relentless. I felt hollow, adrift in a sea of grief with no shore in sight, no solid ground beneath me, only an aching void deep inside my heart.

The trauma lingered, casting a long, unshakable shadow over my life. For years, it followed me—quiet but ever-present, a weight I carried even as I tried to move forward, tried to rebuild, tried to make sense of a world that no longer felt whole.

An Angel Appears

In the midst of this tragedy, one of my mother's sisters, Tia (Aunt) Angelica stepped forward like a beacon of light. A true angel in every sense, she embodied the kindness and strength her name suggested. With calm resolve and gentle strength, she shared with me a promise she had made to my mother long ago. She'd been there for Laura's birth and had stayed close during the terrifying days when Laura had fallen ill with meningitis. My mother, anticipating life's uncertainties, had asked her one thing: if anything ever happened, would she care for Laura as her own?

A wave of relief washed over me as she spoke. I had assumed Laura would come to live with me, and while I would have done anything for her, I knew it would be hard on both of us. Laura had roots—a community, a church, a job, and a network of support for her special needs. How could I provide the stability and care she required while balancing my career and my own healing?

But my Aunt Angelica, with unwavering grace, assured me that Laura belonged with her and her two sons. Even through the haze of grief, I recognized the profound gift she was giving me—the gift of knowing Laura would be safe, surrounded by love, and that I could continue on to pursue my personal and professional dreams. In return, I made a promise to her and to Laura—a promise to support them both emotionally and financially, a commitment I continue to this day, and have held onto with unbreakable resolve, even after Laura's passing from breast cancer in 2004.

A World That Stood with Me

Devastated and exhausted, we had somehow managed to push through the relentless, soul-crushing tasks that tragedy demands. Arrangements had been made, papers signed, impossible decisions faced and carried out. Every step had felt like trudging through quicksand, each task another cruel reminder of what had been lost. We had buried our mother. We had laid our father to rest. We had endured the unimaginable.

But grief is relentless. Even when the logistics are handled, even when the world expects you to move forward, it lingers—pressing in, heavy and suffocating. Each morning, I woke up to the same unbearable truth, and each night, I fell into restless exhaustion, only to repeat the cycle all over again.

And yet, in the midst of that darkness, something extraordinary happened—an unexpected light that cut through the sorrow.

It wasn't something that changed everything. But it was *acts of kindness*—pure, simple, and unprompted. A reminder that even in the face of tragedy, the world could still hold goodness. That not everything was lost.

My colleagues at IBM, people I had known mostly through the professional veneer of the office, had heard what happened to my parents and quietly came together to support me in ways I could never have imagined. They had raised funds, pooling their resources to provide for my sister, and even arranged for a local NM IBM sales rep to drive out to our family home to personally deliver a check for funeral expenses. When he handed me that check, I was overwhelmed. This gesture was as unexpected as it was deeply moving.

A dear friend, without a word, deposited several thousand dollars into my checking account, anticipating the strain of the funeral costs and expenses I had never prepared for. It was as if she had known exactly what I needed. My parents hadn't left any financial cushion—no savings, no checking account to draw from. Covering a double funeral and all the accompanying expenses had drained everything I had. Yet here were these people, offering their compassion and generosity, lifting away the heavy worry of bills and expenses so I could focus on grieving and taking care of what needed to be done.

In those moments, I understood something I hadn't before. Loss didn't erase love. Tragedy didn't destroy kindness. Even in the depths of sorrow, there were hands willing to reach out, to hold, to remind me that I wasn't completely alone.

And in that sliver of light, I found the smallest ember of strength to keep going.

In those bleak days, their thoughtfulness became an anchor—a lifeline I clung to as I tried to steady myself amidst the storm. I'll never forget the wave of relief that swept over me, knowing that in my moment of profound loss, these gestures were like rays of light piercing through a dark, unyielding sea of grief. Their kindness was more than generosity; it was hope, reminding me that even in the depths of despair, I was not alone. These acts of kindness were lifelines, allowing me to focus on grieving without the weight of financial strain.

Finding My Way Back

Once much had been settled in Las Cruces, I returned to my apartment in Menlo Park, numb and burdened by the memories of the tragedy.

When Everything Shatters

Grief clung to me, heavy and unrelenting. I wasn't just exhausted; I was hollow and weighed down by the sheer enormity of it all.

Mechanically, I pressed play on the answering machine, listening to the backlog of phone messages waiting for me. Most were from well-meaning friends offering their condolences, their voices kind but distant, as if unsure how to speak into the void of my grief.

Then, I heard my boss, Kevin's voice from IBM.

There was no pressure, no expectation—only quiet compassion. His words were simple but held a weight that hit me unexpectedly: *Take all the time you need. Don't rush back. We're here when you're ready.*

I hadn't realized how much I had dreaded returning to work until that moment. The idea of stepping back into the world, pretending to function when I was barely holding myself together, had loomed over me like a shadow. I had been bracing myself for it, preparing to force my way through, to slip back into "normal" as if sheer willpower could override grief.

But hearing those words—hearing someone *see* my pain and acknowledge it without expectation—was like permission to finally let go.

I collapsed onto the couch, my body shaking, the dam finally breaking. No more logistics to handle. No more decisions to make. No more responsibilities to shoulder. For the first time since the nightmare began, I wasn't in "task mode."

Finally, I let myself truly grieve. The waves of grief crashed over me, and I didn't fight them. I let them come, let them take me under, because I finally understood there was no way around this pain—only through it.

Allowing myself to feel the loss was searing. The pain was raw, overwhelming, and I was barely holding myself together. IBM had recently launched a program connecting employees with therapists, and in those days, that therapist became my lifeline. I clung to our sessions like a drowning person grasping for a life raft. She didn't have magic words to take away the pain, but she gave me space to say the things I couldn't tell anyone else—the anger, the confusion, the crushing weight of shame and loss. She helped me name the chaos swirling inside me, making it feel, if not manageable, at least not insurmountable because everything reminded me of the trauma; my concentration was shot, and even the smallest tasks felt impossible. Friends came by with food and comfort, but they, too, had to return to their lives.

Grief is lonely, even when you're surrounded by people who care. Because at the end of the day, the world keeps moving, indifferent to the wreckage left behind. People return to their routines, their meetings, their errands, while I remained frozen in place, staring at the broken pieces of a life that no longer existed.

I wanted to move forward. I just didn't know how.

It was in those empty hours, alone, that the weight of it all crushed me. My skin would crawl with the discomfort of solitude, each tick of the clock stretching endlessly. Not being able to tolerate alone time, I created a fragile routine. Therapy became my anchor, and I clung to small routines, tiny rituals that gave me a sense of structure in the chaos. Each morning, I went to a quiet diner—not for conversation, but for the simple comfort of a familiar place. Somehow, the staff seemed to understand my need for solitude. They never pushed, never forced small talk. Instead, they silently welcomed me, guiding me to the same quiet corner each day where I could sit, sip my tea, and exist without expectation.

There was something profoundly healing in that unspoken kindness. In those quiet moments, surrounded by the gentle hum of life moving forward, I found a small sense of grounding. I didn't have to be okay—I just had to *be*. And for now, that was enough.

And thanks to the steady support of friends, I began the tentative process of rejoining life. But I was still fragile—a touch away from breaking, held together by threads that often felt too thin.

Executive Empathy

The executives at IBM gave me something rare and invaluable: the grace to heal on my own terms. They granted me six weeks away from the office, no pressure, no expectations. Even when I returned after the six weeks, they eased me back with light duties, understanding that recovery wasn't a switch I could simply flip.

My friends and colleagues became quiet anchors, helping me rediscover pieces of myself I thought had been lost. I managed to regain a fragile sense of normalcy—enough to show up, to function, to move through the motions of life again. But they reminded me of something more: that beyond the haze of grief, there was still joy, still laughter, still life waiting for me to step back into it.

One afternoon, my boss Kevin suggested we step out to the nearby Stanford Shopping Center—not for a formal meeting, but for an informal chat. It was clear he wanted a setting where he could speak freely, beyond the walls of the office. On a beautiful Palo Alto sunny afternoon, we found a quiet spot and with a cup of tea, he began to speak with a tone that was gentle, yet direct.

He spoke with a depth of kindness that I hadn't realized how much I needed. As he shared how much he missed the vibrant, driven person I'd been before my parents' deaths, it wasn't a reprimand—it was a lifeline. His words didn't accuse or demand; they reminded me of the strength I'd forgotten I had. He gently pointed out how others had stepped in to support me during my grief, and then, with a warmth that felt like a soft light piercing through a fog, he told me he still believed in the person he'd hired—the one who tackled challenges with determination and carried the spark of limitless potential.

What moved me most wasn't what he said, but *how* he said it. He didn't push me to let go of my grief or pretend I was okay. He acknowledged my pain, but at the same time, he urged me to reconnect with the part of myself that had *always* risen to meet adversity. His belief in me was unwavering and genuine, and in that moment, I realized how much I had needed someone to remind me of my own strength.

That conversation became a quiet but profound turning point. Grief isn't something you "get over"—it's something you learn to carry. And I began to see that my path forward wasn't about moving past the loss, but about remembering that I still held within me strength, resilience, and the fire that had driven me long before tragedy struck.

It was incredibly difficult to return to real life, to the ambitious path I had once set for myself. But I came to understand that by not doing so, I would be denying not just my future, but everything I had been through. My grief wasn't a barrier; it was a testament to love, to resilience, to the very things that had shaped me. I realized that standing still wouldn't honor my past—it would trap me in it.

That day didn't erase the pain, but it did something just as important. It marked the beginning of a new chapter—one where I would learn to carry my loss, honor it, but also find my way back to myself.

5 Picking Up the Pieces

With fresh eyes, I noticed the quiet sacrifices my colleagues had made in my absence. One coworker, balancing my deadlines alongside his own wedding preparations, had carried my workload without complaint. Others had taken on late-night projects, ensuring I stayed in the loop without the crushing pressure of the front line. Their actions humbled me—they hadn't just kept the wheels turning; they had created a space for me to heal.

Their silent support reminded me of the quiet strength in community—the way people step in, hold you up, and carry the weight when you can't. But as much as they had steadied me, I had to face an unavoidable truth: grief doesn't stay behind closed doors. It doesn't wait politely for you to deal with it when the workday ends. It seeps in, uninvited, filling the spaces between meetings, sitting on your shoulder during conference calls, creeping into moments where you least expect it.

And yet, beneath the grief, something else remained. Faint but present. A whisper of the ambition that had once been my North Star, still flickering in the distance, waiting to be reclaimed.

Healing wasn't linear. It was halting, messy, unpredictable. But slowly, I began the arduous work of finding my footing again. Therapy became more than just a place to grieve—it became a place to rebuild. To rediscover the resilience that loss had buried but not erased. It wasn't about forgetting or moving on; it was about learning to carry the weight without letting it break me.

Work, with its structure and sense of progress, became my bridge back to some semblance of normalcy. At first, it was just about showing up. Completing tasks. Checking boxes. But as I leaned into the work, something shifted. I began to remember *why* I had chosen this path in the first place. The challenges, the drive, the thrill of solving problems and making an impact—it had never just been about the next promotion or title. It was about proving to myself that I could create, lead, and innovate. That I still had something to offer, something to build.

The roadmap I had once envisioned remained as steep and demanding as ever, but now I carried more than just ambition—I carried grief, anger, and shame. Some days, those emotions felt like fuel, pushing me forward. Other days, they felt like an anchor, threatening to pull me under. But through it all, I made a choice: to keep climbing.

This wasn't just about my career anymore. It was about reclaiming my life. About proving—to myself more than anyone else—that even in the wake of unimaginable loss, I could still lead, still create, still thrive. That even when the future looked different than I had once imagined, it was still mine to build.

Adapting My Skillset

Dedicating myself fully to work, I treated each success not as a milestone to celebrate but as a stepping stone to the next challenge. My friends often pointed out that I rarely paused to acknowledge my wins—I was always focused on what came next. At the time, I didn't see this as a flaw. In my mind, forward motion was the only thing that mattered.

At IBM, I had a front-row seat to a seismic shift in the tech industry—from the dominance of mainframe data centers to the rapid rise of desktop computing. Silicon Valley, the beating heart of innovation, was embracing this transformation at lightning speed. Yet, IBM—steeped in its legacy and guided by leadership in its New York headquarters—remained tethered to mainframes, holding onto the historical success that had defined it for decades. The contrast was stark. The future wasn't being built inside IBM's traditional corridors of power. It was happening all around me. And if I wanted to thrive, I had to position myself within this new wave of innovation.

I began paying closer attention to the sales executives around me. Some clung to the old model, doubling down on selling large mainframe computers despite their waning relevance in Silicon Valley. Others saw the shift and adapted, pivoting toward desktop computing and emerging technologies. While desktop deals came with smaller commissions in the short term, they offered something far more valuable: long-term opportunity.

With a renewed focus and a deliberate effort to channel my energy into growth, I began recognizing patterns in the career trajectories of those around me. The professionals who advanced rapidly, attracted top recruiters, and seamlessly stepped into leadership roles weren't just talented—they were strategic. They anticipated industry shifts and positioned themselves ahead of the curve.

Opportunity wasn't just about skill; it was about alignment. Executive search firms sought out IBM's most adaptable, forward-thinking, and polished professionals—those who had successfully navigated the industry's transformation. These individuals weren't just being recruited; they were being poached for leadership roles in emerging companies. Just as significantly, those who made the leap often reached back, bringing along colleagues they respected, reinforcing a cycle of strategic career mobility.

But no one reached back for me.

It was a sobering realization. I had the talent, the drive, the work ethic—yet I wasn't on their radar. That moment became an inflection point. It forced me to ask hard questions: Why wasn't I being recruited? What was I missing?

The answer became clear: no career roadmap is static. Business conditions shift, industries evolve, and if you don't evolve with them, you get left behind. I realized that the skills that had gotten me this far weren't enough to get me to the next level in this fast-moving industry. The rules were changing. And if I didn't change with them, I would become obsolete.

I considered pursuing an MBA to sharpen my financial and strategic skills, but the thought of balancing school and work while still grappling with the emotional weight of my past felt overwhelming. Instead, I turned my focus to something I saw setting true leaders apart: executive presence and the power of communication.

Success wasn't just about technical expertise. It wasn't just about working hard or even having the right connections. It was about knowing how to present ideas with confidence, clarity, and impact. The people who rose fastest weren't necessarily the smartest or the most experienced—they were the ones who could command a room, inspire trust, and articulate a vision.

If I wanted to step into that next level of leadership, I needed to master that.

I enrolled in public speaking courses and immersed myself in the art of storytelling, determined to transform not just how I spoke, but how I *connected*. I studied great communicators, analyzing what made their words resonate beyond just facts and figures. Watching Steve Jobs of Apple command a room with simplicity and charisma, I saw the profound power of presence. He didn't just present information—he painted a vision, pulling people into the future he wanted them to see.

His message wasn't about technology; it was about *possibility*.

I realized that standing out required more than just delivering results—it meant inspiring others to believe in what *was possible*. As someone who loved math for its clear, definitive answers, this shift in thinking was a completely new challenge. It wasn't just about presenting facts; it was about blending logic with emotion, crafting a story that captured imagination and moved people to action.

This demanded not only a different skill set but also a level of emotional presence that I was still learning to navigate—a challenge that felt both essential and deeply personal.

For years, I had carried my grief privately, holding my emotions in check, focusing on what needed to be done rather than what I *felt*. I had built a fortress around my pain, channeling all my energy into work, productivity, and achievement. On the outside, I was composed, driven, and capable. I had rebuilt my ability to function at a high level, to execute, to deliver results.

But great leaders didn't just communicate *ideas*; they communicated *themselves*. They made people feel something—through presence, authenticity, and connection. And that required a level of emotional openness I wasn't sure I knew how to access anymore.

I had once again become highly functional and productive, but inside, my emotions were still compartmentalized. I had mastered the art of keeping my pain hidden beneath the surface, convinced that vulnerability was a distraction, something to be pushed aside in favor of strength and resilience. But I was beginning to realize that *real* leadership required something more.

It wasn't just about intelligence, skill, or even experience. It was about *presence*—the ability to engage, inspire, and connect in a way that made people want to listen. The kind of presence that made someone more than just a top performer—it made them unforgettable.

And to achieve that, I had to be willing to step outside my carefully constructed armor. I had to learn how to integrate *all* of me—my intellect, my drive, my experiences, and yes, even my pain—into the way I communicated. Not to seek sympathy, but to build trust, credibility, and a kind of leadership that wasn't just effective, but *undeniable*.

I wasn't there yet. But for the first time, I understood the gap between where I was and where I needed to be. *And I knew I wasn't ready to close it.*

And then, one day, I walked into the office to hear news that sent a shockwave through our entire branch office: our IBM branch manager had just been hired as the CEO of a fast-growing tech company.

His leap—from branch manager to CEO—was extraordinary. Almost unimaginable. But knowing him, it made sense. He had presence. He could command a room without arrogance, wield humor to disarm critics, and rally support with a confidence that made people want to follow him. He didn't just work hard—he stood out.

His departure set off a ripple effect. Almost immediately, he began pulling top talent from our branch to join him at his new company.

But I wasn't among them.

That realization hit hard. It wasn't personal, but it was a wake-up call.

I had rallied and once again was a top performer at IBM, yet I hadn't made the kind of impression that made me indispensable—the kind that made someone think, I need her on my team. My work ethic alone wasn't enough. My results weren't enough. If I wanted to be in the conversations that shaped the future, I had to do more than just deliver—I had to be seen.

That moment crystallized something in me. It wasn't just about refining my skills or working harder—it was about stepping into the kind of leader I knew I could become. I recognized the professional skills I needed to develop—executive presence, strategic communication, and the ability to command a room. Those were tangible, actionable goals.

But beneath that realization, there was something else I wasn't ready to face. While I was focused on professional growth, I was still avoiding the emotional weight I carried.

What Gets You Here Won't Always Get You There

That moment became a pivotal lesson: the skills that got me here weren't enough to take me further. It wasn't just about understanding the product or selling a vision—it was about standing out in a sea of talent, showing up with the poise, confidence, and adaptability to lead in a rapidly changing industry.

In Silicon Valley, speed and skill were everything. To make big leaps forward, I couldn't rely on the static roadmap I'd once envisioned. I needed to adjust, learn, and grow. As a trailblazer, I realized that while we may set out on a clear path, the world often changes faster than we expect. It's up to us to adapt, acquire new tools, and ensure we're ready for what lies ahead.

From that day forward, I made a commitment: I wouldn't just prepare for the roles I had—I would build the skills for the opportunities I *aspired* to. Whether it was mastering public speaking, deepening my financial acumen, or staying ahead of industry trends, I began to see every gap not as a weakness, but as an opportunity to grow. Because in a world that moves this fast, standing still isn't just a pause—it's a choice to be left behind.

And I wasn't about to let that happen.

Cue the Tape

After completing introductory speaking classes, I decided to push myself further, taking a leap into an executive-level speaking course. This wasn't an IBM program—it was an elite, high-stakes training designed for executives looking to refine their communication skills and elevate their presence. It wasn't cheap. At the time, spending thousands of dollars on a course that didn't directly tie to my job was a major financial investment. That money could have gone toward any number of practical needs. But deep down, I knew that if I wanted to advance in my career, *good enough* wouldn't cut it.

I needed to push beyond my comfort zone, to see what I was truly capable of when I stepped into spaces that challenged me in new, transformative ways.

The assignment seemed deceptively simple: deliver a compelling three-minute presentation.

Walking into the sleek, glass-walled offices high above San Francisco, I was immediately struck by the sheer presence of the other attendees. These were senior executives from industries I barely understood—finance, biotech, retail luxury brands—each one exuding confidence, polish, and precision. Their tailored suits, practiced gestures, and effortless authority made one thing clear: I still had plenty of room to grow.

But I clung to what I knew. My presentation was solid. My data was airtight. My enthusiasm was genuine. I had delivered plenty of successful pitches at IBM—why should this be any different?

One by one, we stepped onto the stage, our words captured on camera, our every movement under scrutiny. Some presenters were masterful—effortlessly charismatic, drawing the audience in with the kind of presence that made you hang on every word. Others were raw, achingly authentic, their vulnerability making them unforgettable. A few struggled, their nerves visible, their words hesitant.

Then it was my turn.

I took the stage, confident that my energy and command of the facts would set me apart. I believed my passion would shine through, that my knowledge would carry me.

And then came the moment of reckoning.

We reviewed the footage—but this time, *without sound*.

That's when the real lesson hit me.

When my video played, my heart sank. What I thought was captivating energy came across as frenetic. Without words to lean on, my gestures looked erratic, my movements desperate to fill a void rather than commanding presence. I didn't *look* like an executive ready to lead or inspire.

The feedback from the room was unanimous and brutally clear: *I didn't look like someone others would follow. I didn't look like someone whose message they would buy into.*

It was a hard pill to swallow. I had always believed that intelligence, hard work, and preparation were what truly mattered. But in that moment, I realized something else carried just as much weight—*presence*.

Yet, despite how raw the critique felt, it wasn't cruel. It was a gift. These people weren't trying to tear me down; they were holding up a mirror, showing me what I *could* be if I embraced the challenge. They weren't questioning my intelligence or my ability—they were pointing out the unspoken gap between where I was and where I needed to be.

If I wanted to rise to the next level, *good enough* wasn't the target—*excellence* was.

For the first time, I saw the distance I needed to travel. Neutral, unfiltered feedback illuminated weaknesses I hadn't even been aware of, gaps that had likely held me back in ways I hadn't recognized. It wasn't that I lacked the skills or the drive—it was that I wasn't yet fully stepping into the *presence* of a leader.

And presence wasn't about titles, experience, or even the words I spoke. It was about how I carried myself, the energy I projected before I even opened my mouth.

Still reeling from the experience, I made a decision. My goal wasn't just to meet expectations—it was to *surpass* them. Not to simply hold my own in the room, but to redefine what I was capable of. To develop an executive presence that made people stop and listen.

This wasn't just a technical adjustment—it was a transformation. A shift in how I stood, how I spoke, how I *owned* the space around me. It was about learning not just to present, but to *command attention*. Not just to communicate, but to *connect*.

And if I could master that, there would be no ceiling I couldn't break through.

That realization was both *liberating* and *daunting*.

When you are trying something new, especially something that is difficult, you often find yourself walking alone, making sacrifices others aren't willing to make.

The investments—in time, energy, and discomfort—aren't for the faint of heart.

But I remembered something my mother told me years earlier, as I left for my first job at NASA JPL in Pasadena. She had pulled me aside, her voice steady but her eyes filled with tears, and said, "Sometimes being the first in your family to dream big is the hardest thing you'll do. It's lonely, but it's necessary. You have to go where others haven't gone, even if it means sacrifice."

I had understood her words then, but I *felt* them now.

This was one of those moments. I was standing at the edge of something new, something uncertain. And while I was still carrying the weight of grief, still wrestling with the loss of my parents, I knew the work ahead wasn't optional.

This wasn't just about improving my speaking skills. It wasn't just about looking more polished or projecting confidence.

It was about *fundamentally transforming* how I presented myself to the world.

I had a choice—stay where I was, or step forward, even if it meant struggling, even if it meant failing, even if it meant sacrificing my comfort to become the person I *knew* I was meant to be.

And so, I chose to step forward.

Opportunities Disguised as Obstacles

I began applying the lessons from that program, shifting my focus from simply delivering information to *owning* the way I presented it. It wasn't just about what I was saying—it was about *how* I said it. My posture, my tone, my ability to engage an audience—all of it mattered just as much as the content itself.

With this new awareness, I started refining my approach to customer presentations. Instead of just conveying new product information, I reimagined them as compelling narratives—designed not just to inform, but to *influence*. I focused on clarity, confidence, and presence, ensuring that every presentation left a lasting impression.

The difference was noticeable. My delivery became more polished, my ability to hold a room more powerful. I wasn't just passing along details—I was leading conversations, shaping discussions, and positioning myself as someone people listened to. The more I practiced, the better I got, and more of my IBM colleagues began asking for me to help them with their clients.

Then, one day, my phone rang. On the other end was a former IBM colleague—someone I had worked alongside, someone who had seen my growth firsthand. He had moved on to Apple and was now working in product marketing. After some small talk, he got to the point.

"There's an opportunity here," he said. "A role in product marketing. I thought of you immediately. Are you interested?"

The question sent a jolt through me. *Interested?* Of course, I was. This was exactly the kind of opportunity I had been working toward. Years ago, when I had mapped out the experiences I needed to reach an executive role, product marketing had been on that list. This wasn't just another job offer—it was a stepping stone, a pivotal shift in my trajectory.

But beyond the strategy, beyond the carefully crafted career roadmap, there was something else. *Apple.*

In the tech world, IBM was respected—but Apple was *revolutionary*. It was where bold ideas and unconventional thinking thrived. Where creativity wasn't just encouraged—it was expected. The chance to work in that environment, to stretch myself in ways I hadn't before, to step inside one of the most innovative companies in the world, was electrifying.

I had spent years preparing for an opportunity like this. And now, it was here.

"Yes," I said, without hesitation. "I'm interested."

Out of Sync with Leadership

At Apple, I moved quickly—first in the United States and then internationally. Apple was the industry darling, a company defined by growth and innovation, and I embraced that ethos fully. I threw myself into the work, creating opportunities and driving business growth at every turn.

But in my relentless pursuit of success, I sometimes found myself moving faster than my boss's vision or comfort level. My instinct was always to push ahead, to *make things happen*. When my boss reached out to align, I often bristled, interpreting those conversations as obstacles rather than opportunities for collaboration. I saw their concerns as attempts to slow me down, to impose limits when all I wanted was to accelerate.

Instead of addressing the tension, I doubled down on what I knew best—delivering results. I believed that numbers would speak for themselves, that extraordinary growth would override any friction. After all, in a company like Apple, results mattered.

The same pattern repeated when I transitioned into Latin America. I created opportunities at a pace that outstripped my director's vision for the business. I saw untapped potential and moved quickly to capitalize on it. Once again, when my boss expressed concern or tried to rein things in, I took it as resistance rather than guidance. My response? Work harder. Grow the business faster. Let the success of the numbers prove my worth. And they did, posting dramatic growth.

What I failed to see was that results alone weren't enough. Leadership wasn't just about driving growth—it was about alignment, influence, and knowing when to bring people with you instead of charging ahead alone. By focusing solely on outcomes, I had neglected one of the most critical elements of success: managing up. And without realizing it, I was creating a disconnect that would eventually demand my attention.

Looking back now, I see what I couldn't see then: I was standing in my own way. The simmering anger and unresolved grief from my parents' deaths, and especially the anger toward my father, was seeping into my professional relationships, especially with authority figures. I viewed their attempts to align as obstacles rather than opportunities to collaborate, and I responded defensively, creating friction where there could have been trust.

But at the time, I was in a hurry—driven by ambition and a relentless need to prove myself. I didn't pause to reflect, to see the lesson that life kept placing in front of me. Instead, I repeated the same pattern, letting my emotions cloud my judgment and missing the chance to grow in a way that went beyond driving business results.

I didn't fully feel the weight of my actions—or their consequences—because I was too caught up in the rhythm of performing and producing results. My ability to move at the speed of innovation, create growth, and adapt to shifting markets became my defining strength. These skills, combined with a relentless focus on results, became my hallmark.

While the cracks in my relationships with authority figures at work were real, the sheer scale of the business results I was delivering kept propelling me forward. Recruiters began reaching out with offers that promised new challenges and bigger opportunities because they had seen my ability to deliver results, even in extremely challenging market conditions. These calls from recruiters were not just job offers—they were validation. They signaled that my work was resonating and positioning me as a leader capable of driving transformation in an industry that valued decisiveness and results.

When the right opportunities came along, I took the leap. These weren't just promotions or new job titles—they were stepping stones that expanded my impact, sharpened my skills, and propelled me further into the fast-moving, ever-evolving world of technology. Each move felt like forward momentum, proof that I was on the right track.

But when you're in the thick of your career ascent—focused on delivering, achieving, *winning*—there's little time for self-reflection. You don't always realize what you *don't* know. I certainly didn't. I was so intent on proving my value through results that I underestimated the importance of something just as critical: managing relationships, especially with those above me.

Looking back, I can see how those moments of tension with my bosses weren't just obstacles—they were *missed opportunities*. I didn't yet understand how essential it was to continuously strengthen those relationships, to align not just on business goals but on expectations, communication, and trust. At the time, I saw my relentless drive as an asset. But I can see now that my tunnel vision sometimes cost me the chance to build the kind of strategic partnerships that would have made my path smoother.

Beyond the workplace, I was still carrying emotions I hadn't fully processed—grief, ambition, self-doubt—all simmering beneath the surface. And whether I admitted it or not, those emotions shaped my approach, clouding my judgment at times, making me more reactive than reflective. I pushed forward with determination, but I hadn't yet mastered the deeper skills that separate good leaders from great ones: patience, emotional intelligence, and the ability to bring people along with me instead of simply charging ahead.

Yet, with every transition, every setback, and every hard-won success, I added new tools to my arsenal. Each challenge—no matter how frustrating or unexpected—was shaping me, forcing me to confront blind spots I hadn't even realized existed. The lessons weren't always immediate, and at times, I pushed forward without fully understanding the deeper growth taking place. But growth isn't always obvious in the moment.

Brick by brick, the foundation was laid—not as a refuge, but as a battleground. Every postponed choice, every sidestepped truth, had been waiting, accumulating, pressing in around me. The moment was coming when I would have to stand in the thick of it, face-to-face with the lessons I had buried—the ones that had been shaping me in silence, demanding to be reckoned with. But the weight of it all was crushing, and the truth was, I wasn't ready. I simply preferred to avoid rather than deal with the pain.

6 | Succeeding at Failing

There is a Japanese proverb, which succinctly summarized my approach: *Fall Seven Times, Stand Up Eight*. Eager to press forward, I leapt from one opportunity to the next, crafting a career that, on paper, seemed to be progressing. Each move added another layer of expertise—manufacturing, sales, product marketing, international business—bringing me closer to the vision I had once sketched as a checklist for myself. Every step forward wasn't just a promotion; it was another layer of experience that sharpened my ability to navigate the complexities of the tech industry.

But the higher I climbed, the steeper and more unforgiving the lessons became. Two of the most defining chapters of my career—at Autodesk and Dell—were not just about reaching new heights but also about enduring the fall, learning the hard and humbling lessons that only failure can teach.

More Carrot, Less Stick

At Autodesk, I stepped into a career-defining role: leading the Latin American division with full Profit and Loss (P&L) responsibility. It was a position I had meticulously prepared for over the years, a culmination of my experience in sales, marketing, and international business. But it was also *highly unusual*. No other women were leading Latin American operations for a major software tech company at the time. The industry was overwhelmingly male, and Latin America's business culture was no exception. I knew I had to prove myself, not just as a capable leader, but as someone who could deliver real, measurable results in a market many had already written off.

Piracy was rampant across Latin America, so widespread that it had become part of the fabric of the software economy. It wasn't just a nuisance—it was Autodesk's biggest competitor. Our legitimate sales were being gutted by black-market copies, devaluing the product and crippling our potential growth. The scale of the problem became glaringly clear on my very first Autodesk business trip to Mexico. As I slid into the backseat of a taxi, making small talk with the driver, he casually turned around and offered to sell me a pirated copy of our flagship product, AutoCAD—*for a mere fraction of its actual price.*

That moment crystallized the uphill battle ahead. The industry's response to piracy was predictable—punitive measures like lawsuits, cease-and-desist letters, and aggressive legal threats. But those tactics weren't working. Piracy wasn't just a nuisance; it had shaped the very structure of the software market in Latin America. Distribution channels were fragmented, informal, and heavily influenced by black-market sales. Legitimate resellers struggled to compete, and businesses, accustomed to easy access to cheap, unauthorized copies, saw little reason to change.

Most software companies had all but written off investing in Latin America. The region was seen as too saturated with piracy to justify investing in formal sales channels. Instead of fighting an uphill battle, many companies took the path of least resistance, focusing on indirect sales through established hubs in Miami, Los Angeles, or Houston. These cities became unofficial distribution centers, where Latin American businesses would purchase software for their operations back home, avoiding the legal and logistical complexities of the local market.

It was a workaround that kept some revenue flowing—but it also kept companies from truly unlocking the region's potential and from serving multinational customers in the region. And in the process, companies left millions of dollars in untapped opportunity sitting on the table.

But I saw it differently.

Rather than fighting the black market head-on, I focused on making legal distribution the more attractive option. But I didn't do it alone—I had an *exceptional*, can-do team that embraced the challenge with relentless determination. We weren't just executing a strategy; we were driving a fundamental shift in how software was sold in the region.

Having worked in Latin America for years and having strengthened Apple's reseller channels in the region, I knew the market's potential. Global multinational businesses didn't *want* to rely on pirated software; they simply didn't have a viable local alternative. The industry's punitive approach had done little to shift behaviors. Instead of trying to eliminate piracy outright, I saw an opportunity to reshape the market and change the way businesses viewed legitimate software.

Together, we worked closely with resellers to expand their offerings beyond just software, equipping them with advanced training, enhanced technical capabilities, and direct support from some of the top software engineers at Autodesk. We didn't just improve sales tactics—we elevated the entire ecosystem. Our resellers became trusted advisors, offering value-added services, custom applications, and enterprise-level solutions that piracy couldn't replicate.

Beyond commercial success, we forged partnerships with universities and other agencies to showcase the *real* power of AutoCAD. One of our most groundbreaking initiatives was using the software to digitize national heritage sites, including the pioneering work of digitization of the Mexican pyramids at Teotihuacan. These projects demonstrated that AutoCAD wasn't just a tool for business—it was a force for preservation, innovation, and progress.

We also introduced tiered pricing to make legitimate software more accessible, particularly for large enterprises and multinational corporations that prioritized security, reliable updates, and technical support. By strengthening technical expertise, expanding industry influence, and showing the *true* value of our software, we weren't just shifting market perceptions—we were reshaping the future of design technology in Latin America.

This wasn't just about selling products—it was about reshaping an entire market. With a bold mindset and a willingness to challenge the status quo, my team and I took on what others had deemed impossible. And in doing so, we achieved something extraordinary.

By shifting the conversation from *enforcement* to *value*, we changed the equation. Businesses no longer saw purchasing legitimate software as a forced compliance measure—they saw it as a strategic advantage.

The results were extraordinary.

Under this new model, resellers didn't just survive—they *thrived*. Equipped with deeper technical expertise, expanded service offerings, and a compelling business case, they became trusted partners to enterprises that had previously relied on pirated software. The shift wasn't driven by fear of lawsuits or enforcement—it was driven by *value*.

Large corporations across Latin America began transitioning to legitimate software purchases, not because they were forced to, but because it simply made *business sense*. They needed reliability, security patches, and access to technical support—critical factors that pirated software could never provide. More importantly, they saw Autodesk as more than just a software vendor; we became an essential partner in their growth, offering cutting-edge tools, training, and expertise that elevated their capabilities.

Then, something *unprecedented* happened.

In one record-breaking quarter, Latin America accounted for more than *half* of Autodesk's total profit. This wasn't just a financial win—it was a complete paradigm shift. It proved that even in the most challenging markets, transformation wasn't just possible, it was *inevitable* with the right strategy. Latin America, long dismissed as a piracy-ridden region with limited potential, had become a powerhouse of growth for the company.

For me, this was more than just a validation of our strategy—it was *personal*. I wasn't just leading a division; I was proving that bold thinking, persistence, and a willingness to challenge conventional wisdom could reshape not just a business, but an *entire industry's* perception of what was possible in Latin America.

This success wasn't just about revenue growth or market share—it was about rewriting the narrative. It was about showing that even the toughest markets could be transformed with a bold vision backed by real insight and relentless execution. Where others saw insurmountable obstacles, we had seen opportunity. And together, my team and I had turned that vision into reality.

The energy was *electric*. I had built an extraordinary team, and we were operating at a level where everything clicked. It was one of those rare moments in a career when the work didn't just feel *rewarding*—it was *exhilarating*. Strategy, execution, and momentum had aligned perfectly, and the results spoke for themselves. We had turned Latin America from a piracy-laden challenge into a thriving, high-growth market, and in the process, I had cemented my place as a leader who could drive real transformation.

Riding the wave of what felt like unstoppable success, I felt *invincible*. But just beyond the horizon, a hard lesson was waiting—a lesson that would challenge everything I thought I knew about confidence, preparation, and humility.

Blindsided

One day, my boss called to confirm the forecast ahead of an upcoming earnings call. I didn't hesitate. "We're golden," I said, my voice steady, my confidence unwavering. I had no reason to doubt. We had delivered win after win, my team was performing at an extraordinary level, and the momentum was undeniable.

What I *couldn't* see—what *no one* foresaw—was the storm brewing just out of sight.

Before the quarter closed, everything changed.

Mexico unexpectedly devalued its currency, sending shockwaves through the world economy. Overnight, what had been a forecasted profit transformed into a loss—one so significant that it didn't just hit my division; it reverberated across the entire company's financial performance. The numbers I had once delivered with unwavering confidence had crumbled, and the weight of that collapse landed squarely on my shoulders.

But it wasn't just the financial impact that hit me—it was the *personal* sting of falling short after such a streak of victories. I had been soaring, executing at the highest levels, proving what was possible in a region that many had dismissed. And then, in an instant, I was knocked back down. The confidence I had relied on so heavily—*the belief that I had everything under control*—was shaken to its core.

And when my boss called to address the fallout, I didn't handle it well. I got *defensive*. My frustration bubbled over as I scrambled to justify what had gone wrong. It was an economic crisis, an external force beyond my control! I couldn't see the situation clearly because my pride was in the way. Instead of taking full ownership or focusing on solutions, I pushed back—blinded by the sting of the loss and the bruises to my ego. I let my emotions cloud what should have been an opportunity to lead through adversity.

At first, the failure consumed me. I replayed the events over and over, looking for what I had missed, wondering how I could have anticipated the blow. Had there been warning signs? Could I have prepared differently? The endless questioning was brutal, but as time passed, the real lesson became clear.

Response, Recovery, and Resilience

It wasn't just that I had underestimated external risks—I had also failed to build resilience into my strategy. I had been so focused on *driving growth* that I hadn't adequately considered how to *protect* it. But even more than that, I realized that leadership wasn't just about making the right decisions when things were going well—it was about how you respond when things fall apart.

And in that moment, I had failed to respond like a leader.

My inability to rise above the emotional sting of failure didn't just strain my relationship with my boss—it cast a shadow over how my leadership was perceived. People weren't just looking at the loss; they were looking at how I handled it. And in that, I had let myself down.

The hard truth was unavoidable: setbacks are inevitable. But how you respond to them defines your credibility as a leader. It can either fortify your reputation or shatter it.

The lesson was clear: true leadership means focusing on solutions, not shifting blame. It requires taking full ownership—no matter how unfair, unexpected, or frustrating the situation may be. It's about composure, grace, and the ability to lead forward, even when everything feels like it's falling apart.

This wasn't just a financial loss—it was a wake-up call. Confidence, while powerful, has to be tempered with caution and humility. Real leadership isn't just about celebrating the wins; it's about owning the losses, recalibrating, and coming back stronger. I had spent too much time caught up in the sting of failure, but eventually, I had to face the reality that replaying the past wouldn't change it. So, I got over myself. I let go of my defensiveness, stopped fixating on what had gone wrong, and shifted my focus to what actually mattered—fixing the problem.

Together, we took a hard look at what had happened, not to assign blame, but to ensure we were better prepared for the future. We analyzed financial vulnerabilities, reexamined our forecasting models, and built strategies to insulate the company from future currency fluctuations. We put safeguards in place so that a single economic shift wouldn't catch us off guard again.

This wasn't just about recovering from a setback; it was about fundamentally changing how we operated. We developed contingency plans that strengthened our financial resilience—not just in Latin America, but across all global markets.

The lesson had been painful, but it forced me to grow. Setbacks aren't just obstacles to endure—they're opportunities to improve. I had started out as part of the problem, but by embracing the challenge instead of resisting it, I became part of the solution. Most importantly, it taught me that humility in success is just as vital as resilience in failure.

Dell Paves My Path to Austin

My accomplishments at Autodesk in Latin America—even in the wake of the Mexican peso's collapse—didn't go unnoticed. Executive recruiters had taken note, and in 1997, I was approached by Dell, a company experiencing a meteoric rise. Dell wasn't just expanding; it was transforming, evolving from a dominant force in desktop computing into a major player in enterprise technology. They were looking for leaders who could bridge the gap between marketing strategies and enterprise product solutions, and I was brought in to help drive that vision forward.

This role was different. It demanded not just execution, but imagination and partnering with the different departments all focused on the new Dell Server products. This position required the ability to see around corners, to anticipate where the industry was headed, and to craft strategies that positioned Dell as an indispensable partner for large-scale enterprise customers. It was high-stakes, high-speed, and exactly the kind of challenge I wanted.

The energy at Dell was undeniable. Decisions were made fast, bold ideas were embraced, and the company thrived on momentum. It was a place where execution mattered more than talk, and results were the ultimate measure of success. In that high-stakes, fast-moving environment, I thrived. My team and I took on the challenge of working with other internal teams to crystalize how to convey Dell's position in the enterprise space. One of the most groundbreaking initiatives was a bold campaign to position Dell's servers as the backbone of its entire enterprise business—Dell on Dell.

For years, Dell had been known primarily as a PC company, dominating the personal computing space but rarely considered a serious contender in enterprise technology. Many industry leaders dismissed Dell's ability to handle the demands of large-scale businesses, assuming its servers weren't built for mission-critical workloads. The company's reputation was rooted in efficiency, affordability, and direct-to-consumer sales—not in powering the infrastructure of global enterprises.

That perception needed to change.

The strategy was simple yet powerful: prove Dell's enterprise capabilities by showcasing the ultimate use case—Dell itself. At the time, Dell was one of the fastest-growing, most admired companies in the world, a Wall Street and industry darling. The company wasn't just expanding—it was scaling at an extraordinary rate. And what was running this high-growth, multibillion-dollar business? Dell's own servers.

The message was clear: if Dell's technology was powerful and reliable enough to handle the demands of its own complex, global operations, then it could meet the needs of any enterprise customer.

Dell on Dell wasn't just a marketing campaign—it was a proof point that shattered old assumptions. It forced the industry to take a second look, shifting Dell's reputation from a PC company to a legitimate enterprise powerhouse.

Dell had always been a company that bet on speed and scale, but now, it was proving that it could dominate in enterprise technology just as aggressively as it had in personal computing.

In the late 1990s and early 2000s, Dell's server business skyrocketed, crossing the $1 billion milestone in record time. It wasn't just a financial win—it was proof of the power of vision, strategy, and fearless execution by the entire company.

From Experiment to Breakthrough

At the same time Dell was aggressively targeting enterprise customers, I saw an opportunity in another market for servers: power users—engineers and designers—who craved server-level performance on their desktops.

Having just worked at Autodesk, I had seen firsthand how architects, software engineers, and other technical professionals pushed their machines to the limit, desperate for more computing power than a standard desktop could provide. I had walked into offices where desktops were stacked with extra hard drives, where PCs were crammed with expanded memory, all in an effort to stretch beyond their hardware's original capabilities. These users didn't want a data center—they wanted enterprise-grade performance on their desks at their fingertips. Yet this market wasn't part of Dell's original server strategy.

Internally, there was resistance. The consumer sales team didn't want to push high-priced servers to end users, fearing sticker shock. Meanwhile, the major accounts team worried about losing control over enterprise customers if individual employees started purchasing outside of corporate agreements. The idea of selling servers directly to power users was unconventional, and no one wanted to take the risk.

Finally, we brought the idea to the Dell.com online sales team, pioneers in selling custom personal computers through an online store. They were open to the experiment but knew we had to manage expectations to not impact the consumer or enterprise business. They came up with a way to test the market. A limited pilot—only over a three-day holiday weekend. And there was a catch: If a customer actually placed an order for a server, someone from my team had to be on call to handle the inquiry. Dell was wary of investing in building and shipping expensive server products only to have them returned by customers experiencing buyer's remorse because of the cost.

As the director of the team, I took the first shift on that Friday night. Not long after the server site went live, an order came in. It was a large purchase, thousands of dollars—far more than the typical Dell.com transaction. Per our agreement, the customer was instructed to call Dell before the order could be processed.

I took the call, prepared to explain the high cost and make sure they understood exactly what they were buying. Before I could get far, the customer cut me off, clearly agitated.

"Yes, I know how much it costs. That's why I'm ordering online—I don't want to talk to anyone. I know exactly what I need, and I just want to buy it."

The same scenario played out repeatedly. Within hours, the Dell.com team managers saw the pattern: These customers weren't hesitant—they were *highly informed*. They had done their research, they knew exactly what they wanted, and they didn't need anyone to walk them through the purchase. The pushback from other departments was not true for this customer. Instead of scaring off buyers, the online model *enabled* them.

That weekend changed everything. We had unlocked an entirely new customer segment—one that was not only lucrative but exceptionally self-sufficient. Power users eagerly embraced the ability to configure high-performance servers tailored to their unique needs, bypassing the traditional sales process altogether.

What started as an experiment turned into a breakthrough. It didn't just validate our approach; we had unlocked an entirely new customer segment—one that was not only lucrative but exceptionally self-sufficient. Power users eagerly embraced the ability to configure high-performance servers tailored to their unique needs, bypassing the traditional sales process altogether.

With these wins under my belt, I walked into my performance review confident that my work spoke for itself. I had not only exceeded expectations but had been instrumental in the effort to position Dell as a serious competitor in enterprise computing and championed an entirely new market for power users, proving that enterprise-grade technology could be sold directly to individuals.

I had expected my boss, who had been very supportive, to just know the full scope of my contributions. I didn't make sure he had the information he needed to advocate for me. I had assumed that my results would speak for themselves and that recognition would naturally follow. That was my mistake.

I wasn't just hoping for it—I was certain I had earned it. A promotion, additional stock options, a clear step up—something that reflected the impact I had made. Instead, I walked out with a raise, a bonus, and a solid performance review. But no stock. No title change. No major next step.

When I pressed for more specifics, my boss looked at me and said, "I wish you had mentioned all of this before the review. I could have gotten you some stock, but not a promotion." I sat there, stunned.

The message was clear: my work had been valuable, but not enough to warrant advancement. Yes, I was part of Dell's incredible enterprise server success, but when it came to my own career progression, I had somehow been left standing still. And I had no one to blame but myself.

I had failed to communicate. I had made it harder for my boss to advocate for me, to articulate my impact in a way that secured the incentives I deserved.

The Language of Leadership

Walking out of that review, my confidence was rattled. Had I misread my own impact? Had I failed to position myself for advancement? What was I missing? I had delivered results—big ones. But as I replayed the conversation in my head, I realized that in my relentless focus on execution, I had overlooked something critical. Success in a fast-moving company wasn't just about driving business growth—it was about making sure leadership saw me as an integral part of the company's future, not just a high performer. I had been so focused on delivering, on proving my ideas worked, that I hadn't fully considered how I was being perceived at the leadership level.

I could either let this moment define me as someone who was good at execution but not seen as a strategic leader—or I could use it as fuel to redefine my path. I had broken barriers, reshaped markets, and driven millions in revenue. Now, it was time to do the same for my own career.

The disappointment was sharp, but what stung more was the realization that I had failed to advocate for myself. I had assumed that results alone would be enough, that my work would speak for itself. But I had made a critical mistake—I hadn't framed my impact in a way that resonated with leadership. I had delivered growth, but I hadn't positioned that growth as essential to the company's larger strategy.

Frustrated, I turned to a trusted colleague on Dell's executive team, looking for clarity. She listened carefully before delivering a perspective I hadn't considered.

"It's not just about results. In a company growing this fast, everyone is hitting their numbers—that's the baseline. What sets leaders apart is showing how their work drives strategy, scales profitably, and aligns with the company's bigger vision. That's the 'value add' executives recognize."

Her words hit me hard. I had spent years pushing toward the executive level, proving my ability to drive business success. But in that pursuit, I had overlooked something fundamental—I hadn't been speaking the language of the senior executive leadership.

In my relentless focus on execution, I had framed my contributions in terms of outcomes, not strategy. I had failed to articulate how my work fit into the company's long-term vision, how it created scalable, sustainable value, or how it strengthened Dell's competitive position. While I had been working at the highest levels of execution, I hadn't yet positioned myself as a strategic leader.

Executives weren't just looking for results—they were looking for leaders who could think beyond their own wins, who could connect their work to the company's financial and strategic objectives, and who could demonstrate they understood not just how to drive growth, but how it mattered in the broader scope of the business.

I had been so focused on proving I could execute that I had failed to prove I could lead at the next level. Operational execution was expected—leaders at the executive level weren't rewarded for just delivering results; they were valued for shaping strategy, driving long-term growth, and ensuring the company remained competitive.

Executives didn't hire peers to execute their plans; they hired people who could create the plans. They looked for leaders who understood the broader business landscape, who could connect their work to financial impact, market positioning, and sustainable value creation.

I realized I wasn't just competing on performance—I had to show that I understood the business of the C-suite. I needed to communicate that I could think beyond my own lane, that I had the vision, strategic thinking, and leadership perspective to contribute at the highest levels.

It wasn't enough to prove I could drive success. I had to prove I could shape the future of the business itself.

Upward vs. Outward

Armed with this new perspective, I began to shift how I communicated my contributions at Dell. Instead of simply reporting on what my team had achieved, I reframed our work to highlight its strategic impact. I connected our successes to Dell's larger goals—profitability, scalability, and market positioning—ensuring leadership saw our initiatives as integral to the company's long-term growth.

When I presented to executives, I no longer just shared metrics; I told the story behind the numbers. I demonstrated how our work not only delivered immediate results but created opportunities for the future. I positioned our wins as stepping stones toward broader company objectives, aligning my team's efforts with Dell's vision in a way that was impossible to ignore.

The results were undeniable. My ideas gained traction, executive buy-in became more consistent, and my reputation as a strategic thinker strengthened. Yet, despite this progress, it still didn't lead to a promotion.

When I moved into a new division, I found myself facing a familiar challenge—outpacing alignment with my director. I was delivering results, driving growth, and seeing success, yet my relationship with leadership remained strained. A pattern was emerging: I excelled at execution but still struggled with leading upward as effectively as I led outward.

That realization hit hard. It wasn't just about the work; it was about navigating power dynamics, building trust, and ensuring that my ambitions were aligned with the priorities of those above me.

I could sense I was on the brink—so close to the long-dreamed-of, hard-fought ascent to the C-suite. I had the experience, the results, and the momentum. So why hadn't I reached that level yet?

The answer wasn't just professional—it was deeply personal. My experiences at Autodesk and Dell didn't just reveal gaps in my approach; they exposed something far more profound. I had been carrying emotional baggage that shaped my career in ways I hadn't realized. The anger from my parents' tragic deaths had wired me to see many in authority as obstacles rather than allies, turning collaboration into a battle instead of a shared mission. Leadership wasn't something I aligned with—it was something I challenged.

At the same time, shame lurked beneath the surface, keeping me from fully stepping into my worth. No matter how many wins I had, a part of me still hesitated to claim my value, to advocate for myself with the same confidence I used to drive business results.

This wasn't just about learning a new leadership skill—it was about unlearning the patterns that had held me back.

For the first time, I saw my career not just as a series of achievements, but as a mirror reflecting the deeper work I needed to do. If I wanted to break through, I had to stop seeing leadership as something to fight against—and start seeing it as something to step into.

The battlefield wasn't in the boardroom. It was in me.

Reaching the C-suite would take more than results. It would require a reckoning with myself. Success wasn't just about execution—it was about relationships, influence, and making sure my contributions weren't just recognized, but positioned as essential to the company's future.

The journey to the C-suite wasn't just about what I needed to do. It was about who I needed to become.

Moving Forward

Failure isn't just part of the journey—it defines it. Success isn't a straight line or a smooth climb; it's a relentless cycle of falling, learning, and rising again. Each failure can be a stepping stone, but only if you choose to see it that way. For too long, I had seen setbacks as barriers, roadblocks that slowed me down. But I began to realize they weren't stopping me—they were shaping me, forcing me to grow into the leader I needed to become.

It wasn't enough to deliver results. It wasn't enough to win. Success wasn't just about the work itself; it was about ensuring that work was seen, valued, and understood. It was about stepping out of the shadows of execution and into the spotlight of influence. It required trust—trust in myself, trust in those around me, and trust that leadership wasn't a fight to be won, but a mission to be shared.

But before I could build that trust with others, I had to confront the hardest truth of all—I didn't fully trust myself.

For years, I had carried the weight of my past, burying my anger, my shame, my grief beneath relentless drive and ambition. I had convinced myself that sheer force of will could push me past any challenge, that results alone would be my voice. But the deeper I looked, the clearer it became: the greatest barrier wasn't external. It was me.

I had to face what I had long avoided—the anger that made me see authority as an adversary, the shame that kept me from fully embracing my own worth, the defensiveness that shut out those who could have lifted me higher. These weren't just emotional scars; they were the invisible hand shaping my decisions, my leadership, my career. And they had held me back for too long.

I couldn't power through this. I couldn't outwork it. The only way forward was through.

To become the leader I aspired to be, I had to stop fighting the pain from my past and start owning my future. Because the truth was clear—no title, no promotion, no external success would ever be enough if I didn't believe, deep down, that I deserved it.

And so, I stopped running.

I stopped resisting.

I faced it all.

And for the first time, I saw that the path ahead wasn't just about reaching the top.

It was about becoming the person who belonged there.

7 | Forgiveness

Forgiveness

This chapter is the turning point—the moment I had to face my biggest obstacle: myself.

For anyone who feels stuck, repeating patterns they can't escape, this is the work that matters most. It's about confronting the unspoken struggles, unveiling vulnerabilities, and reconciling truths that have long been avoided. This internal reckoning is what determines whether you move forward or remain circling the same ground.

The struggle to forgive—especially when the pain runs deep—isn't about excusing the past. It's about releasing the grip it has on you. It's about understanding that learning the lesson and stepping back to rebuild isn't the same as giving up.

When I left Dell, I carried with me a long list of lessons and accomplishments, but I couldn't ignore the truth staring back at me. Despite my success, I had not reached the level of leadership and fulfillment I had envisioned. It would have been easy to blame others—to point to senior leadership decisions, corporate politics, or structural limitations. But a deeper realization cut through the noise.

I had worked at several companies, and the same issue followed me. My performance was always excellent. My results spoke for themselves. But my ability to cultivate the relationships that would propel me to the next level was lacking.

For years, anger and defiance had been my fuel. They pushed me forward, drove me to prove every doubter wrong, and made me relentless in my pursuit of success. But defiance isn't the same as purpose. And survival is exhausting.

More than a decade had passed since my parents' deaths, and the weight of it all finally caught up with me. I couldn't outrun the truth any longer. The common denominator in my frustrations, in my limitations, in the walls I kept hitting—was me.

It was a dawning, uncomfortable realization. The patterns holding me back weren't just the result of circumstances or other people. I had been setting limits on myself without even realizing it. And that acknowledgment was the first crack in the armor I had worn for so long.

To truly move forward, I had to do more than achieve. I had to be vulnerable. I had to face my emotions, my family history, and the deep wounds I had buried beneath relentless overachievement. I had to stop running from the anger that had become my shield, the shame that had taken root in my soul, and the grief I had spent years avoiding.

And hardest of all, I had to learn to forgive—not just others, but myself.

Only when I stopped running, when I turned to face the shadows, the emotions, the grief, could I begin to understand what it meant to truly live.

Looking back, I see how my defiance had become its own kind of prison. Fixating on proving others wrong meant I wasn't building a vision for myself. I wasn't asking what I truly wanted, who I wanted to become, or what a meaningful life looked like beyond success. Instead, I was letting anger and resentment set my course. And while that fueled remarkable achievements, it left me feeling empty.

I had an entire room in my home dedicated to my career trophies—plaques, medals, awards that reflected my relentless drive. But standing among them, a familiar, gnawing question always crept in: What's next?

Each accolade brought a moment of pride, but no trophy or award could fill the void I carried inside. It wasn't authority figures I needed to defy—it was the self-imposed limits I had placed on myself.

Stepping back to rebuild wasn't about giving up. It was about finally doing the work that mattered—the work that would allow me to move forward, not just with success, but with a heart freed from pain and anger.

The Weight of Anger

My anger wasn't loud. It didn't explode in dramatic outbursts or fiery confrontations. Instead, it simmered quietly beneath the surface—a slow, relentless burn. It wasn't directed at the people I loved; it found its target in those who held authority. Managers, executives, anyone who seemed to wield power over my life became the focus of my distrust. I bristled at their directives, silently questioning their motives and daring them to underestimate me. My defiance was my armor, and I wore it proudly, ready for battle at every turn.

At the time, I couldn't see it for what it was. This anger wasn't about them—it was about me. It was the anger of a daughter grappling with the unbearable loss of her parents in the most violent way imaginable. It was the anger of a professional woman navigating a field where no one looked like her, where every step forward was hard-fought and hard-won. It was the anger of someone who had learned to survive but hadn't yet learned how to heal.

That anger gave me an edge. It made me relentless, a fighter who refused to be underestimated. It fueled my drive, pushing me to work harder, prove myself again and again, and never back down. In the toughest moments, it gave me the resilience to keep moving forward. But what I failed to see was that the same defiance that had once been my greatest weapon was now becoming my greatest obstacle.

It wasn't strength—it was a wall. A fortress I had built to shield myself from vulnerability, disappointment, and rejection. It protected me from pain, but it also kept me from growth.

What I didn't realize was that this wall wasn't just keeping others out—it was keeping me locked in. It isolated me from the alliances, mentorships, and relationships that could have accelerated my growth. I had mistaken resistance for resilience, independence for leadership. I saw compromise as weakness and authority as something to challenge rather than collaborate with.

This wasn't just a mindset—it was a self-imposed limit disguised as strength. And it would take years before I truly understood how much it was costing me.

The Burden of Shame

If anger was my armor, shame was the chain around my neck—unyielding, heavy, and suffocating. I carried it silently, burying it so deeply that no one could see how profoundly it was entwined with my sense of self. Yet, it was always there, an invisible weight that influenced my every decision and interaction. The trauma of my parents' deaths had etched itself into my very being, anchoring me in a state of perpetual vigilance.

Workplace discussions about holiday plans put me on edge, knowing that an innocent question about visiting parents could send me into an emotional tailspin. Casual conversations about family became minefields I learned to navigate carefully, dodging any mention of my parents to avoid the painful reality of explaining how they had died so young—and at the same time.

Losing a family member is always a profound loss, but when that loss is violent and traumatic, it cuts deeper, leaving wounds that feel impossible to heal. The weight of it never fully lifts; it lingers in the spaces where normal conversations should be easy, where others speak of their parents without hesitation, while I hesitated, calculating how to steer the discussion away from my own truth.

On the rare occasions I did share my story, I stumbled under the enormity of it, never sure how to explain it without making it feel *too much*—too raw for me, too overwhelming for others. And when I did confide in someone, it never felt like a release. Instead of unburdening myself, I felt as if I had placed the weight of my grief on them, as if I had forced them to carry a piece of the shame I had carried alone for so long.

The fortress I had built to contain the pain didn't just shield me—it isolated me. Shame and grief became my silent companions, shaping how I saw myself and dictating how much of me I allowed others to see. They formed an unspoken barrier between the life I was living and the life I desperately wanted to embrace.

This emotional weight didn't just hold me back—it tethered me to an unrelenting fear that everything I built, everything I loved, could vanish in an instant. Loss had come for me before, swift and merciless, and some part of me was always bracing for it to happen again.

What I didn't yet understand was that breaking free wouldn't come from working harder, achieving more, or proving myself to the world. It would require something far more difficult. I had to confront the shame, unravel the stories I had told myself, and find the courage to forgive—not for anyone else, but for myself. I had to stop building from fear and start rebuilding from a place of acceptance, strength, and the belief that I was worthy of something greater than survival.

The Turning Point

The turning point came when I finally faced a truth I had long avoided. After yet another missed opportunity, my business coach—someone I had hired to help me navigate my career—offered me the kind of blunt honesty I didn't realize I needed.

"You're brilliant," she said, her tone direct but not unkind. "But you're holding yourself back. It isn't about work. It isn't about your boss. It's about what's inside of you. You need to find a therapist."

Her words struck like a lightning bolt, cutting through the layers of defensiveness I had built over the years. In that instant, I began to see my anger and shame not as weaknesses but as signals.

Anger wasn't just an emotional response—it was a neon sign pointing to where I felt powerless. Shame wasn't simply a shadow I carried—it revealed the wounds I needed to heal. These emotions weren't barriers to be ignored or suppressed; they were guideposts, directing me toward the deeper work I had spent years avoiding.

For so long, I had believed that pushing forward, achieving more, and proving myself would silence these feelings. But no amount of success could outrun what lived inside me. And for the first time, I realized that healing wasn't about getting rid of these emotions—it was about understanding them.

Desperate for answers, I turned to books, searching for language to make sense of what was happening within me. One book on PTSD (Post-Traumatic Stress Disorder) stood out. As I flipped through its pages, the descriptions mirrored my own experiences with eerie precision. The hyper-vigilance. The need to over-prepare for every possible outcome. The fear that everything I had built could vanish in an instant. It was all there, spelled out in stark clarity.

Reading those words felt like holding up a mirror to my life. I had spent years thinking I was simply wired this way—relentless, intense, always bracing for the worst. But now, I saw it for what it really was. These weren't just personality traits or quirks. They were the lasting imprints of trauma.

That realization was both terrifying and freeing. For the first time, I could see my behaviors not as personal failures, but as survival mechanisms. My drive, my discipline, my relentless work ethic—they had all been shaped by a deep-seated need to control what felt uncontrollable. I wasn't just ambitious. I was trying to outrun the past.

But now, I had a choice. I could continue living this way, letting trauma define my path, or I could finally start to unpack it. Not by suppressing my emotions, not by pretending they didn't exist, but by listening to what they were trying to tell me.

Because maybe the way forward wasn't about proving anything. Maybe it was about healing.

Seeking Help

Living in Austin, I began researching therapists who specialized in trauma and PTSD. After some searching and some recommendations, I found someone and made an appointment. But even then, the thought of addressing the pain that had been simmering beneath the surface for so many years was almost too much to bear.

When the day of the appointment arrived, I drove to her office and parked my car. The building was unassuming, with a set of external stairs leading to her second-floor office. I sat there in my car, staring at the stairs, my heart racing and my palms clammy. Every instinct screamed at me to turn the key, drive away, and pretend this moment had never happened.

But something deeper—a quiet feeling beneath the noise of fear—urged me to move forward. One step at a time, I got out of the car and walked toward the stairs. My legs felt heavy, each step deliberate and plodding. When I reached the door to her office, I hesitated, my hand hovering over the handle. I wasn't just opening a door—I was bracing myself to confront the sharp, relentless pain I had carried for years. The idea of exposing this agony to myself and another person was almost too much to bear. I pushed the door open and stepped inside. It was the first step in a journey I didn't yet fully understand, but I knew one thing with certainty: I was ready to stop running. Ready to face what had kept me trapped for so long.

Learning to Be Self-Aware

I was fortunate to have the personal support to focus on my healing, but no amount of preparation could lighten the weight of what lay ahead. The road to confronting my past was uncharted territory, and every step felt uncertain. My therapist, a specialist in trauma recovery, urged me to start with small but crucial steps—breathing exercises to calm my nervous system and shift my perspective. But how could I shift something so deeply ingrained? This pain ran so deep, it felt like an undeniable truth, not just an emotional wound.

One session stands out in stark clarity. I made an offhand remark, spoken with the certainty of someone who believed it to be law: "All fathers are detached and unloving." It wasn't a question. It wasn't up for debate. It was a fact, or so I believed.

My therapist didn't argue. She didn't push back. Instead, she gave me an assignment that seemed almost laughable in its simplicity: "Notice fathers with their children. Just observe. At a park, in a store, on your street—pay attention to their interactions."

I scoffed, brushing off the idea as pointless. What difference would it make? But I wasn't someone who left a task undone, so I agreed. Begrudgingly, skeptically—but I agreed.

What I didn't realize was that this assignment would be the first crack in a belief I had held for far too long.

That afternoon, I drove to Austin's Town Lake with my dogs, the familiar loop around the water offering its usual refuge. Walking there had always been a way to clear my mind, a place where I could move without thinking, letting the rhythm of my steps drown out the noise in my head.

As I pulled into the parking lot and opened the door to let the dogs out, a scene unfolded just a few spaces down. A man was carefully unloading a kayak from the roof of his car, his two young children bouncing with excitement beside him. "Don't forget your life preservers," he reminded them, his voice steady and warm. As he set the kayak in the water, he explained what they might see—frogs, fish, a hidden cove perfect for a picnic. His words were patient, thoughtful, effortless. But it was his tone that stopped me in my tracks—calm, kind, full of care.

I stood frozen, watching.

I didn't expect to feel anything, yet something in me shifted. I watched them paddle away, their laughter carried over the water, and a strange sensation rippled through me. It wasn't a thought, but something deeper—a feeling, a stirring, as if a door long sealed inside me had just shifted open. Not easily, not smoothly, but like a rusted lock being forced to turn after years of neglect.

As I continued my walk, I noticed more fathers. One was crouched at the water's edge, showing his son how to skip stones. Another held the back of his daughter's bike, steadying her as she wobbled forward, her determination fierce and his encouragement unwavering. These weren't isolated moments. They were everywhere.

By the time I returned to my car, I was carrying more than the dogs' leashes in my hands. I was carrying the weight of something I hadn't realized was missing—the beginning of a new understanding.

The following week, I recounted the experience to my therapist. I barely made it through the first sentence before my voice broke. The words caught in my throat, tangled with a flood of emotions I hadn't been ready to face. And then, the tears came—heavy, unrelenting, years in the making.

For so long, my father's final act had eclipsed everything else about him, burying his memory beneath layers of pain and shame. But now, through this simple exercise, something else began to surface. Moments I hadn't allowed myself to remember. Pieces of him that had been lost in the shadow of his last decision.

I remembered the time I stumbled out of the sixth-grade spelling bee, humiliated after being eliminated in the first round. My father didn't chastise me or diminish my feelings; instead, he sat beside me and said, "Everyone has a bad day. It doesn't mean you're not smart." Or the time I was denied a car loan after my college graduation, despite having a job. My father said, let's go to the bank together, and declared to the loan officer, "Why are you denying my daughter a loan? Let's see the paperwork." I drove home in the new car.

And then there were the stories from his coworkers. Every time we ran into one, they would pull me aside, eager to share how proud my father was of me. He drank his morning coffee at work from a "Proud Stanford Dad" mug, telling anyone who would listen that his daughter went to Stanford. It was a small thing, but it wasn't. It was a declaration, a quiet but steady proof of his love.

As these memories poured out, my heart cracked open—not in despair, but in a way that made room for something I hadn't allowed myself to feel in years: healing. My father wasn't perfect. He carried burdens I would never fully understand. But he did love me. And more than that, he was proud of me.

All I had ever wanted was his approval, his belief in me. And as I sat in that therapist's office, years removed from my youth, I cried—not just as the little girl who had longed for his validation, but as the woman who finally realized it had been there all along.

I wiped my tears, trying to collect myself, when my therapist said softly, "When the way you look at things changes, then what you look at changes."

Those words landed with the weight of a revelation. The past hadn't changed—but maybe, finally, I was ready to see it for what it really was.

Fresh Eyes

This shift wasn't just about seeing my father differently—it was about reclaiming a part of myself I hadn't even realized was lost. For years, shame had held me captive, shaping how I saw the world and myself. But as the weight of it began to loosen, something profound happened. The pain I had buried no longer felt like an immovable wall—it became something I could face, piece by piece.

In seeing my father as complex, flawed, and deeply human, I unknowingly began to extend that same grace to myself.

That simple exercise did more than soften my heart—it fundamentally reframed how I saw the world. Healing, I realized, isn't about grand gestures or sudden revelations. Transformation happens in the small, deliberate shifts in perspective, the moments when we choose to see with clarity and compassion instead of fear and resentment.

One of the most powerful lessons I learned was that the space between a reaction and a response is where real growth happens. It's in that pause—when we resist the urge to lash out, retreat, or shut down—that we have the opportunity to choose differently. To choose understanding over anger. To choose reflection over reactivity. To choose healing over hurt. It's where we can breathe, step back, and choose not to react from fear, anger, or shame, but from a place of intention and calm.

For anyone carrying their own weight of pain, fear, or doubt, know this—you don't have to fix everything at once. Healing doesn't come in a single, triumphant moment. It comes in the quiet decisions you make each day: the choice to look at something differently, to sit with discomfort rather than numb it, to ask questions instead of assuming answers. Each small shift brings you closer to a version of yourself that isn't defined by past wounds but by resilience, strength, and hope.

The path may feel uncertain, but step by step, it leads you somewhere new—a place where the unimaginable becomes possible, and where you begin to see yourself not as broken, but as whole.

My life didn't change overnight. Healing isn't linear. It's painstakingly slow, and the pain is very real. My therapist helped me unpack decades of emotions, one layer at a time. Some days, it felt like too much—too exhausting to endure, too overwhelming to believe a hopeful outcome was even possible. But as I kept digging deeper, I began to see the tangled roots of my family's past. Loss, survival, unspoken grief—it wasn't just my burden to carry. It was something that had shaped all of us, passed down in ways I had never fully understood.

Slowly, I began to recognize the patterns—how generational trauma had woven itself into my family's story, influencing our choices, our fears, our silences. For the first time, I saw that I wasn't just trying to heal myself. I was trying to break a cycle.

I began to see my father with new eyes—not just as the towering, authoritative figure of my childhood, but as a man shaped by the absences and wounds of his own past. His quiet stoicism, his reluctance to express love or praise, wasn't just who he was—it was the armor he had built over a lifetime. Beneath that exterior was a man who had learned early on that love could be conditional, that fathers could leave and start new families, that abandonment could be a defining force. His father had done exactly that—walked away from his first family to create another family, leaving behind a fractured family and a son who would spend his life trying to prove he was worth staying for.

My mother's story was different, yet in many ways, it echoed the same painful theme. The second daughter of 13 children, she grew up in relentless poverty, her childhood shaped by survival rather than innocence. Her mother's first husband died young, leaving her a widow with several children to feed. When she later became pregnant by another man—my mother's father—he disappeared entirely, leaving yet another void in a home already stretched beyond its limits.

But my mother didn't crumble under the weight of hardship. She became the glue that held her family together, transforming scarcity into sustenance, struggle into strength. Where others saw impossibility, she found a way. She wasn't just resilient—she was resourceful, a force of sheer will. Yet, as I learned in my own journey, survival comes at a cost. It's exhausting to always be strong, to always carry more than your share. And for my mother, that burden only grew heavier after my sister Laura's life changed following her illness.

My parents' histories, though starkly different, shared a common thread: the absence of a father's daily presence. For my father, it was a source of shame and yearning, an emptiness that made him seek validation in his work and his role as a provider. For my mother, it was a wound she refused to acknowledge, a void she filled with self-reliance and defiance. She never spoke of her father with longing—only with anger. She told us he was dead, and only later did I learn he had not died. When I confronted her, she replied without hesitation, "He's dead to me."

Together, my parents carried invisible burdens—loss, anger, longing, and shame—passed down like an inheritance neither of them had asked for. They had survived their pasts, but they had never fully healed from them. And as I looked deeper into their stories, I began to understand something I had never truly grasped before: I wasn't just carrying my own pain. I was carrying theirs, too.

As I traced these threads, the story took an improbable twist, one that felt as if fate itself had woven it.

One Side Plundered, the Other Rewarded

My paternal great-grandparents had once been wealthy landowners in Chihuahua, Mexico. Their lives, steeped in privilege, were upended when Pancho Villa's forces descended upon their lands. Knowing they were vulnerable—Protestants in a predominantly Catholic region—they fled the night before a raid, taking only what they could carry and boarding a train bound for the Juarez-El Paso border. Behind them, they left everything: their ranch, their bakery, their livestock.

For my great-grandparents, the loss was more than financial—it was the shattering of a legacy. My great-grandfather never fully recovered. In El Paso, he found work at a grocery store, far from the independence and prosperity he had once known. My grandmother, my father's mother, carried that bitterness with her, mourning not just lost possessions but the life that could have been. She often spoke of the coming-out party that never happened, the elocution lessons she no longer could take, the horses she had to leave behind, the land that became a distant memory.

Then came the revelation that bound these histories even closer. An old photograph—grainy and sepia-toned—captured Pancho Villa reclining in a wealthy landowner's car, parked in the courtyard of a home he had seized. Beside him sat his bodyguard, a man who, improbably, was my maternal grandmother's cousin. That courtyard? It was rumored to be the very home my paternal grandfather's family had fled.

On one side of my family, Villa was the destroyer, the thief of futures. On the other hand, he was a benefactor. The wealth he had seized—silver coins hastily poured into a sack for my maternal great-uncle, my grandmother's uncle—became an unexpected lifeline, offering my maternal grandmother's family a brief reprieve in desperate times. The irony was almost too cinematic to believe. A revolutionary who had stripped one side of my family of their home and given the other a chance at survival.

These stories—woven together like an intricate tapestry—became a powerful reminder of life's contradictions. History is never clean, never simple. It is filled with unexpected intersections, with moments of loss and survival, with villains and heroes who sometimes exist in the same breath.

What had once seemed like two separate narratives—my father's family, stripped of their land and legacy, and my mother's family, finding a fleeting lifeline in the very same upheaval—were, in fact, bound together. The same revolution that shattered one lineage had, in a twist of fate, sustained another.

Each thread of my family's past carried something deeper than just hardship or triumph. It carried the weight of choices made in moments of crisis, the resilience to rebuild after devastation, and the inescapable truth that history is rarely as black and white as we wish it to be.

These contradictions didn't cancel each other out; they enriched the story. They made me see that no legacy is singular, no family's past is one-dimensional. Instead, each piece—whether marked by suffering, perseverance, or unexpected fortune—was part of a larger, more complex whole.

And in that complexity, I found something more profound than just understanding. I found a new way to see my own journey—not as a straight path, but as one shaped by the resilience and survival of those who came before me.

This realization transformed me. For years, I had worn anger like armor, believing it protected me from pain when, in reality, it only kept me trapped inside it. Anger had given me an edge, a way to push forward, but it had also isolated me, hardening me against emotions I wasn't ready to face. But as I connected the pieces of my past—my parents' struggles, their burdens, the weight they carried long before I was even born—I began to see forgiveness not as surrender, but as freedom.

It wasn't about absolving or excusing. It wasn't about pretending the pain wasn't real. It was about breaking free from the resentment that had bound me for too long. Forgiveness wasn't about them—it was about me. About releasing the grip the past had on me so I could finally step into the life waiting ahead.

One morning, in the quiet solitude of my home, I sat down and wrote letters to each of my parents. At first, the words poured out in anger—anger at my father for what he did, for shattering our family in an instant. Anger at my mother for staying, despite the warning signs I could now see so clearly in hindsight. But as I wrote, something unexpected happened. Beneath the anger, grief surfaced—raw and aching, a pain I had buried for years. And beneath that grief, love emerged—not uncomplicated, not without scars, but love nonetheless.

I wasn't erasing the pain; I was transforming it.

This was the real work of moving forward—not running from the past, but learning from it. Accepting its lessons, carrying its weight in a way that no longer crushed me but shaped me into someone stronger, wiser, more whole.

As I neared the end of each letter, I hesitated, my pen hovering over the final words. And then, with a deep breath, I wrote the sentence I had never believed I could: *I forgive you. And I love you.*

The words weren't easy. They weren't perfect. But they were honest.

And then, in an act as deliberate as it was necessary, I burned the letters. I watched as the flames consumed them, turning years of anger, grief, and unspoken words into smoke and ash. As the last pieces curled and disappeared, I felt something lift—a weight I had carried for so long I had forgotten what it felt like to be free of it.

In that moment, I wasn't just letting go of the past. I was reclaiming my future.

And for the first time, I felt light. The weight of generations, of pain passed down, of wounds never spoken aloud—it was no longer mine to carry.

Breaking free from the patterns and emotions that hold us back isn't about erasing the past—it's about transforming it. It's about taking what once felt like an unbearable weight and reshaping it into something that fuels growth instead of pain.

When I finally stopped running and turned inward, I discovered a new kind of strength—one not forged in defiance, but in purpose. The hardest battles we fight are the ones within ourselves, and only by facing them can we step into a life no longer dictated by wounds, but shaped by possibility.

This was my turning point, and it can be yours too: a life no longer bound by resentment, but built on resilience. A life where the past no longer dictates the future, where strength is not measured by resistance, but by the willingness to heal.

This wasn't just the start of a new chapter. It was the start of a life unbound—free from anger, untethered from shame, and finally open to the quiet, steady power of grace.

8 | Turning Point to Take Off

The moment I began to see the world differently, it was as if a weight had lifted—a shift so profound it was almost disorienting. For years, anger and shame had fueled my drive, pushing me forward but also keeping me trapped in a cycle of proving, fighting, and surviving. But as I let go of that burden, something new took its place: possibility.

For the first time, my future wasn't dictated by my past. The road ahead was no longer just about overcoming struggle—it was about building something bigger. Hope. Purpose. Vision. I wasn't just reacting to circumstances anymore; I was stepping forward with intention, choosing to create rather than simply endure.

For most of my career, I believed success followed a straight line—one leading directly to the C-suite through sheer determination and execution. But life had other plans. As I learned to pivot with purpose, I realized that the dream I had been chasing wasn't tied to a single, rigid path. The goal hadn't changed, but the way I would reach it was nothing like I had expected. And in that pivot, I found something even greater than personal achievement—I found purposeful impact.

This chapter is where those lessons turned into action. What started as a personal transformation began to take shape in real, measurable ways, reaching beyond me to positively benefit students, families, and entire communities.

Through education, collaboration, and a relentless focus on creating opportunities, I saw how even the smallest, most intentional efforts could spark lasting change. What began as a local initiative in Austin—helping bridge gaps in education and creating workforce pathways for young people—quickly gained momentum. I collaborated with schools, community leaders, and organizations, witnessing firsthand how access to knowledge and opportunity could change the trajectory of a life.

But change doesn't happen in isolation. As the work expanded beyond Central Texas into Los Angeles and beyond, it became clear that the barriers students faced weren't just local—they were systemic. And with each step forward, the scale of what was possible grew larger than I had ever imagined.

What I hadn't anticipated was where this path would take me. What began as grassroots efforts evolved into opportunities to shape public policy and influence national conversations. Before I knew it, I found myself in spaces I had never imagined when I first sat down to help a single child with reading. From Central Texas to the White House, from local classrooms to leading the Girl Scouts of the USA, what once felt like a detour had become a journey of impact—one that extended far beyond what I had ever envisioned.

And through it all, one undeniable truth emerged: when you create opportunities for others, you don't just change their path—you expand your own. With every step forward, new opportunities emerge, revealing possibilities you never knew existed.

By stepping off the expected path and embracing opportunities aligned with a deeper purpose, I discovered that I could arrive at the very place I'd been striving for all along—not in spite of the pivot, but because of it.

Goldfish

It started with what seemed like a simple request: a neighbor asking if I could volunteer an hour a week to help students with reading at a local elementary school. I agreed, thinking it would be a small contribution. But that single hour became a pivotal turning point.

I was paired with a shy six-year-old girl. Her quiet demeanor hinted at something more, and in addition to struggling with reading, she also had issues with dental hygiene. Determined to make a small difference, I returned the next week with Goldfish crackers for our session and also a toothbrush and toothpaste. After we finished reading (and snacking), I gently suggested we brush our teeth together. She hesitated but eventually joined me, offering a promising yet timid smile.

The following week, she came without her toothbrush. Undeterred, I brought another one, along with more toothpaste, encouraging her to make brushing a regular habit. This became our routine—reading, snacking, and brushing our teeth. Week after week, I continued to bring new toothbrushes, hoping to instill a simple but meaningful habit.

Then, during our sixth week together, she surprised me. As I arrived, she proudly held out her toothbrush. "You remembered!" I said, thrilled by her progress. Her quiet reply, "Now everyone in my family has a toothbrush."

Her words pierced through me. Something so basic, so fundamental, was a luxury for her family. I shared the story with her teacher, a woman who was no stranger to the challenges her students faced. She nodded, then asked, "Do you have $35?" Surprised, I asked why. She explained, "One of the students broke his glasses, and his family can't afford to fix them." Then, gesturing to the classroom, she added, "Every child here needs something—glasses, dental care, books, supplies. It's always something."

I handed her the $35, but her words stayed with me long after I left her classroom. How could such fundamental needs go unmet? How had these challenges become so pervasive yet invisible to so many? Determined to understand, I started with the data and what I found was bleak. It painted a picture of rising poverty, widening gaps in education, and a workforce unprepared for the demands of a rapidly evolving global economy. The outlook was grim, yet within those statistics, I saw something else—a story of untapped potential.

What began as an hour of volunteering turned into a revelation. At first, it seemed simple—helping one child with reading, offering guidance where I could. But as I listened, observed, and engaged, I saw more than just individual struggles. I saw systemic gaps—barriers that weren't about intelligence or potential, but about access, opportunity, and support. And once I saw them, I couldn't look away.

This was a pivot I hadn't planned for, but one I couldn't ignore.

Forgiveness and gratitude had been deeply personal milestones, but I began to understand they weren't just about my own healing—they were the foundation for everything that came next. Letting go of resentment had cleared the path for something bigger: purpose.

And gratitude had shifted my focus from what I had lost to what I could give.

With this renewed perspective, clarity emerged—an unshakable commitment to creating meaningful impact. My next phase was no longer just about personal achievement; it was about contribution. It was about taking everything I had learned—resilience, intentionality, and the ability to turn vision into action—and using it to open doors for others.

The very skills that had driven my success in business became the driving force behind my educational work, proving that transformation isn't just about what we achieve for ourselves, but about what we build for those who come next.

At first, I struggled to reconcile this shift with the ambitious career path I had spent years building. My focus had always been singular—achieve, execute, advance. Every decision had been weighed by how far it could propel me forward. But something had changed. The success I had worked so hard for no longer felt like the final destination—it felt like a tool. And tools are meant to build something.

This realization was both exhilarating and unsettling. *I had spent my entire career believing that progress meant climbing upward, but now, it felt like it meant reaching outward.* It wasn't just about personal milestones anymore; it was about impact. It was about recognizing the gaps—the unseen roadblocks that kept others from opportunities I had fought so hard to reach—and choosing to do something about them. Not out of obligation, but because I had the power to make a difference.

I thought about all the moments I had been underestimated, the barriers I had broken through. And I realized that for so many, those barriers weren't just obstacles to overcome—they were dead ends. Not because of a lack of talent or drive, but because no one had ever shown them another way forward.

That was the moment I redefined success—not just by what I achieved, but by what I made possible for others.

And so I leaned in. I took the very skills that had fueled my career—strategic thinking, problem-solving, relentless execution—and directed them toward something bigger. I wasn't walking away from my past achievements; I was expanding their purpose. The same determination that had helped me thrive in the corporate world now fueled my commitment to creating access where it had once seemed impossible.

This shift wasn't just about me. It was about seeing differently—understanding that sometimes the most unexpected pivots don't take us off course. They take us exactly where we were meant to be all along.

Answer Your Calling

Living in Austin, a city brimming with potential to become a global tech hub, I began to see a larger puzzle coming into focus. Companies like Dell, AMD, Applied Materials, and others were thriving, driving economic growth and innovation at an unprecedented pace. However, while companies were booming, the very talent pipeline needed to sustain that growth was being left behind. The disconnect was stark.

Where others saw an impossible challenge, I saw an untapped opportunity. This wasn't just about education—it was about forging a bridge between potential and opportunity. The future workforce couldn't be built elsewhere while local talent was left behind. For the region to thrive, we had to ensure that the people who lived there had a pathway to be part of it.

In my journey of healing, I had read all of Dr. Maya Angelou's books. At this moment, a saying of hers echoed in my mind: "When you get, give. When you learn, teach." I wasn't an educator, but I had spent years solving complex problems, aligning people and resources toward a common goal, and driving transformative results. The same strategic thinking that had fueled my career could be applied here. Her words weren't just wisdom; they were a call to action.

I realized that success in business had given me more than just personal achievements—it had given me tools. And now, it was time to use them for something greater. It was time to step beyond the confines of corporate success and channel my experience into impact, not just for an organization's bottom line, but for those in the rising generation.

Reshaping What Is Already There

The moment I began to reimagine the world around me, the pieces of a much larger puzzle started to fall into place. My vision wasn't about building something entirely new from the ground up—it was about transforming what already existed. It was about recognizing potential where others saw roadblocks, about reshaping systems so that opportunity wasn't a privilege for a few but a foundation for many.

This became my guiding principle: meaningful change doesn't always require starting over. More often, it's about rethinking, refining, and optimizing what's already in place. It's about identifying the overlooked, unlocking hidden potential, and aligning resources to meet the demands of today while anticipating the challenges of tomorrow.

But this approach required a fundamental shift—not just in strategy, but in perspective. Real change wasn't about dismantling systems entirely; it was about reshaping them, influencing them, and driving them toward something better. It demanded collaboration, persistence, and the ability to see beyond limitations to possibilities. Progress wasn't just about identifying what was broken—it was about transforming what existed into something stronger, more effective, and built for lasting impact.

The same neighbor who had first asked me to tutor, recognizing my growing involvement, introduced me to Austin's school superintendent, Dr. Pat Forgione. When Dr. Forgione asked me to co-chair the Austin Independent School District's Boundary Taskforce, I saw more than just a civic duty—I saw a chance to turn vision into action. This wasn't just about redrawing lines on a map; it was about shaping a school system to better serve students, families, and communities.

I immersed myself in the work, visiting over 100 schools, walking neighborhoods, and listening to the parents, teachers, and students whose lives would be directly impacted by these decisions. It wasn't just about policy; it was about people—their hopes, their challenges, and their futures.

One of the most meaningful moments in this journey was working alongside former Texas Governor Ann Richards to open a groundbreaking new school in Austin. As part of the Young Women's Prep Network, founded by Texas philanthropists Lee and Sally Posey, we transformed an existing middle school into a public school for young women, spanning middle through high school. This wasn't just about repurposing a building—it was about creating a place where young women could chart bold futures, develop leadership skills, and step confidently into opportunities that had once felt out of reach.

Honoring Ann's Vision

Ann Richards had a gift—not just for leadership, but for seeing potential in others before they saw it in themselves. When she invited me to join the board of the Ann Richards School for Young Women Leaders, it wasn't just about serving; it was about building something that would outlast us all. She had an extraordinary ability to see potential in people before they saw it in themselves, nudging them toward opportunities with her signature mix of grace and tenacity. She wasn't just building a school; she was shaping a legacy for generations.

For six years, I was deeply involved in the school, especially in the critical year before the school opened, working closely with the remarkable principal, Jeanne Goka. There were doubters—people who questioned whether Ann's vision of a school that achieved academic excellence could truly reflect the entire demographic population of Austin. Ann's vision was bold, and we were determined to bring it to life.

Turning Vision into Reality

Selection was by lottery, but families had to apply first, and that meant relentless outreach. I met with parents, attended community events, and worked alongside leaders like Nora Comstock of Las Comadres to ensure that every family, no matter their background, saw this as an opportunity within their reach.

Unfortunately, Ann passed away in 2006, a year before the school opened. In our last conversation, she said, "Sylvia, I believe in you. You can deliver the students to the school that will mirror Austin's demographics."

Her words became my promise. And when the lottery results came in, we had done exactly that—the school became the only school in Austin that truly reflected the city's full economic, geographic, and demographic population.

Walking the Talk

Principal Jeanne Goka often reminded me that leadership wasn't about just holding a title—it was about showing up. I took that to heart. These young women needed more than encouragement; they needed proof that their dreams were possible. I wasn't just a board member of the school—I was an active participant with the students. I shared my journey—from Stanford to NASA to a career in technology—answering their questions with the same honesty and encouragement I once needed. I spoke at events, visited classrooms, and even brought in a bicycle to break down engineering principles in a way that made learning tangible. Every interaction, no matter how small, was an opportunity to show them that their future wasn't defined by their circumstances—it was shaped by their ambition and willingness to reach for more.

An Enduring Legacy

Under Jeanne's leadership, the Ann Richards School exceeded all expectations. It consistently ranked among the top high schools in Texas and the nation, proving that Ann's vision wasn't just aspirational—it was achievable. Today, the school continues to empower young women to lead, thrive, and dream without limits.

Ann once said, "Ginger Rogers did everything Fred Astaire did, but backwards and in high heels." That's exactly what these girls have done—rising to challenges, defying expectations, and proving that with vision, persistence, and action, anything is possible. I was honored to be part of the journey in bringing the Ann Richards School for Young Women Leaders to life.

Social Capital

Dedicating myself to improving educational outcomes wasn't just a project—it was a mission to strengthen the workforce and build a future where local talent could thrive. I worked alongside some of the most dedicated education leaders in Austin, not just solving immediate challenges but reimagining a system that connected students to opportunity and that aligned education with industry needs. Along the way, I met others who shared this vision—leaders who refused to accept the status quo and saw change not as a distant ideal, but as something within reach. What began as a local initiative grew into something far greater, proving that when bold ideas meet relentless determination, transformation isn't just possible—it's necessary.

The relationships I had built over the years, the trust I had earned, and the networks I had cultivated became some of the most powerful tools in my grassroots educational work. It wasn't just about strategy or execution—it was about leveraging those connections to bring the right people together, align resources, and open doors that otherwise might have remained closed. I began to understand that lasting change wasn't just driven by good ideas; it was fueled by the ability to rally people around a shared vision and turn ideas into action.

Unlike many who were overwhelmed by the scale of the problem, my business background gave me a different perspective. I had spent years developing and executing solutions that scaled, and I knew that no challenge—no matter how daunting—was insurmountable if approached with the right mindset. The issues weren't abstract policy debates; they were tangible, fixable barriers that stood between children and their potential.

Fortunately, two other female engineers in Austin also found their way into educational leadership—Susan Dawson, a Princeton-educated engineer and the visionary CEO of E3 Alliance, and Kathrin Brewer, a Berkeley-educated engineer who led Austin Partners in Education. Like me, they had spent their careers solving complex problems in the business world, and they approached education with the same analytical rigor and results-driven mindset. We saw inefficiencies not as inevitable, but as challenges to be solved. We understood that systemic transformation wasn't just about passion—it was about execution, structure, and scale.

These weren't minor inconveniences—they were barriers that stood between a child and their future. A student struggling to read simply because there were no books at home. A child squinting at the chalkboard, not because they didn't care, but because they needed glasses. A child missing school because of untreated dental pain—something entirely preventable yet devastating to their education.

I had spent my career solving complex challenges in the business world, scaling solutions to drive impact. Now, I was applying that same mindset to something even more profound—ensuring that a child's potential wasn't dictated by circumstances but unlocked through opportunity. With every barrier we removed, I saw firsthand the undeniable power of what happens when bold ideas are met with relentless action. This wasn't just about helping individual students; it was about changing the trajectory of entire communities—one problem solved, one opportunity created at a time.

From Challenge to Opportunity

Many educational organizations in Central Texas had well-established programs, but their infrastructure and services no longer reflected the region's changing demographics. Too often, there was a misconception that families and students weren't engaged or interested in education, when in reality, the programs simply weren't designed in a way that was accessible, relevant, or beneficial to them. Many organizations recognized the disconnect but didn't know how—or why—they should adapt.

I saw an opportunity to shift the narrative. Instead of focusing on what wasn't working, I built a compelling business case for why improving educational outcomes was essential to the region's economic future. The workforce of tomorrow wasn't an abstract concept—it was already here, sitting in classrooms across Central Texas. Even a small increase in high school graduation rates would have a direct impact on economic prosperity, attracting employers and strengthening the region's competitive edge.

To make the connection between education and economic opportunity undeniable, I partnered with the call center industry to show, in real terms, how higher graduation rates directly fueled job creation and regional prosperity.

This wasn't about abstract policy discussions—it was about aligning the needs of local employers with the untapped potential of students, transforming what was often dismissed as a social issue into a powerful economic driver.

For many families, the most immediate and compelling motivator wasn't the distant promise of a long-term career—it was the tangible difference between earning minimum wage and securing an entry-level job that paid five dollars more per hour, plus benefits. That single shift could mean the difference between struggle and stability, between living paycheck to paycheck and building a foundation for the future. It provided access to healthcare, financial security, and a stepping stone toward even greater opportunities.

For others, the realization hadn't yet clicked that college degrees and industry credentials weren't just aspirations—they were essential passports to higher-paying jobs in an increasingly digital and automated workforce. The challenge wasn't just about making these pathways available; it was about making them visible, understandable, and within reach.

This wasn't just about aligning a fragmented system—it was about breaking cycles of limited opportunity. It was about showing students and families that education wasn't an abstract ideal but a direct path to better jobs, greater security, and a stronger future—for them and for Central Texas as a whole. Investing in students wasn't just the right thing to do—it was the key to unlocking the region's full economic potential.

At first, skeptics were everywhere, doubting that education and workforce development could truly be connected in a way that created meaningful opportunities for all of the students of the rising generation. But when donors and funders of local educational nonprofits saw a clear, actionable plan—one that linked stronger educational outcomes to better jobs and a more competitive workforce—the conversation shifted. What once seemed like an abstract challenge became an undeniable opportunity. Suddenly, investing in students wasn't just about education; it was about fueling economic growth, strengthening communities, and ensuring Central Texas remained a place where local talent could thrive.

This shift in perspective ignited a sense of urgency. Education was no longer seen as just a philanthropic cause—it was recognized as a strategic investment in Central Texas's economic future. No longer content with outdated models that didn't reflect the region's evolving demographics, funders and decision-makers became committed to aligning resources with the real needs of students and employers. The focus turned from maintaining old systems to building pathways that could drive real, lasting change.

With this newfound clarity, momentum surged. The focus shifted from slow, incremental change to bold, scalable solutions designed to equip students with the skills and opportunities needed to fuel the region's economic growth. What had once been seen as a challenge was now recognized as an opportunity—one that demanded swift, strategic action.

If You Build It, They Will Come

The Feria Para Aprender (The Learning Fair) was born from this mindset. It wasn't just an event; it was a transformative reimagining of how the existing educational system could better serve families. The goal wasn't to invent a new infrastructure but to refine and elevate what was already there, ensuring that families—no matter their starting point—had the tools, guidance, and confidence to navigate the US educational system. In doing so, the Feria became a bridge, connecting families to the possibilities that education could unlock for their children and their futures.

What set the Feria apart was its unwavering focus on simplicity and purpose. Parents, often overwhelmed by the labyrinth of the educational system, stepped into a space thoughtfully crafted to meet them exactly where they were. Educational providers weren't just exhibitors—they were trained to engage meaningfully, bridging gaps with empathy and clear communication.

Every detail was intentional. Color-coded layouts guided families with ease, bilingual resources broke down barriers, and volunteers greeted attendees with warmth and clarity, transforming what could have been an intimidating experience into one of connection and possibility.

The Feria was designed as an immersive, educational journey—much like an IKEA store, but for navigating the school system. Families entered through the Pre-K section and followed a structured pathway through K–12, eventually reaching college and career opportunities. Upon arrival, each family received a passport and age-appropriate books for their children. More than just a keepsake, the passport guided them through every stage of the educational journey, encouraging them to collect stamps as they explored key milestones. The experience emphasized the critical role of early learning and progressed step by step, ensuring that families walked away with a clear understanding of how to support their child's education from early childhood to future career pathways.

This wasn't a passive walkthrough—it was interactive. At each station, families engaged with nonprofits, schools, and resources tailored to the challenges and opportunities of that educational phase. Representatives stood ready, not sitting behind tables, inviting families into conversations. They wore college shirts and spoke with conviction, introducing families to the possibilities of higher education and career pathways. High school stations highlighted critical choices—like electives and career tracks—that prepared students for success. Post–high school areas showcased technical education programs, community colleges, and universities, presenting tangible paths to well-paying careers in fields like engineering, healthcare, and public service.

One of the Feria's most memorable features was the Visualization Station, where children could select a career—astronaut, engineer, lawyer, doctor, teacher, and more—and leave with a personalized photo of themselves in that role. Watching their faces light up as they held those pictures was unforgettable. It wasn't just about imagining possibilities; it was about believing those dreams were within reach.

Before families exited, they stopped at the Commitment Area, a long stretch of paper where parents and children wrote their educational goals. Bold promises like "I will be the first one in my family to go to college," "I will become a doctor," or "I will support my child's dreams" lined the walls, turning abstract aspirations into public declarations of hope and determination. This simple yet powerful act cemented the Feria's impact, leaving families inspired and resolute.

The Feria also included hands-on activities that brought education to life. STEM and robotics demonstrations captivated students, while vision vans provided on-the-spot glasses, ensuring no child's learning was hindered by poor eyesight. Dental kits addressed a critical health need, and the resources distributed over the years—more than 250,000 books, 25,000 dental kits, and much more—left a lasting mark on families and the community.

The impact was undeniable. University researchers, including the Annette Strauss Institute in Austin, tracked the Feria's outcomes and uncovered something remarkable: parents who attended became 94% more engaged in their child's education. This wasn't just an event—it was a catalyst for change.

Other communities took notice, most notably in Los Angeles, where Cal State Dominguez Hills partnered with Univision to bring the Feria to their campus. What began as a local initiative expanded into an event that reached tens of thousands of families, ultimately earning Univision an Emmy for Community Leadership.

But these weren't just numbers or accolades—they were proof of transformation. They represented families taking ownership of their futures, parents stepping into their roles as advocates, and communities coming together to rewrite what was possible. The Feria didn't just inform—it inspired, equipping families with the confidence and tools to shape their children's destinies.

By strategically aligning existing resources with a clear vision, we turned confusion into clarity and challenges into opportunities—delivering results that were not just impactful but truly transformative.

This wasn't a one-time success; it was proof that lasting change doesn't always require reinventing the wheel. By strengthening and reimagining what was already in place, we demonstrated that with vision, collaboration, and persistence, real progress is possible—and sustainable.

My years in the corporate world had prepared me for more than just navigating markets or leading teams. They had taught me to see potential where others saw barriers, to build coalitions around shared goals, and to communicate ideas in ways that sparked action. These weren't just business strategies—they were the foundation for driving meaningful, lasting change.

The Big Leagues

The moment arrived—ready or not.

Everything I had done—creating a shared vision, preparing communities for the future workforce, building collaborative relationships, and leveraging social capital—had led to this pivotal step. When your work starts making an impact, people take notice. What I hadn't anticipated was that our work in Central Texas had reached beyond city lines, beyond state borders, and into the highest levels of the nation. Then came the call: an invitation to serve on the White House Commission on Educational Excellence for Hispanics.

This wasn't just an honor—it was a chance to take the lessons I had learned through experience and apply them on a national scale. The challenges I had seen firsthand in Austin weren't unique; they were woven into the fabric of communities across the country. Now, the stakes were higher, the reach was broader, and the opportunity to create lasting change was monumental.

This wasn't about politics. It was about the future. It was about ensuring that the next generation had the skills, preparation, and self-determination to drive America forward.

Shortly after my appointment, a fellow Stanford alum, Stuart Burden, offered advice that would shape my approach: "The Federal Government is massive. To make an impact, pick one thing and give it everything you've got. Spread yourself thin, and you'll accomplish nothing."

His words resonated. Reflecting on my own journey—the struggles I had witnessed, the opportunities that had shaped my life—I knew exactly where to focus. Programs like Head Start had been a game-changer for so many children, including me.

Determined to make the most of this moment, I committed myself fully. If I was going to make a difference at the national level, I would do it by championing the foundation where everything begins: early childhood education.

Dr. Eduardo Padrón, Chair of the Commission and a visionary leader who had earned the trust of both Democratic and Republican administrations, tapped me to chair the Early Childhood Subcommittee of the White House Education Commission. The mission was clear yet ambitious: identify a single transformative policy that could change the course of early childhood education in the United States. The stakes were immense—this wasn't about minor policy adjustments; it was about unlocking opportunities for millions of children by ensuring they had access to quality education from the very start.

To drive real change, expertise wasn't enough—we needed bold partnerships that could turn vision into action. But the path forward was anything but easy. Resistance was everywhere. Critics dismissed the data, clinging to unsupported beliefs that English immersion was the only viable path to fluency. They ignored the overwhelming research proving that dual-language education was the most effective way for children to become fluent faster in English while maintaining critical cognitive advantages. The battle wasn't just about policy; it was about overcoming deeply ingrained misconceptions.

Then, unlikely allies stepped forward. The Department of Health and Human Services, which oversaw Head Start and other early childhood programs, recognized that these reforms could dramatically improve educational, and *health*, outcomes for millions of children. The military, with its decades-long investment in linguistic training to strengthen national security, understood firsthand the strategic advantage of having trained military personnel natively fluent in English and another language. Their support helped reframe the debate—not just as an education issue, but as an economic and national imperative.

Armed with this coalition, we moved with urgency. The goal was clear: help children achieve English fluency more effectively by using their native language as a bridge. This was about harnessing a child's native home language as an asset, a tool for deeper understanding and faster mastery of English.

We weren't just pushing for a curriculum change—we were challenging an outdated system that ignored both research and the realities of a global economy. Around the world, business leaders operate seamlessly in multiple languages; yet in the United States, rigid policies were stifling that same potential. Studies have proven that when children learn in both their native language and English, they don't just catch up—they excel. They develop sharper cognitive skills, achieve higher literacy rates, and gain the confidence to thrive in a world where being bilingual isn't a barrier, but a competitive advantage.

And this wasn't just about individual success—it was about America's future. A multilingual workforce strengthens national security, fuels economic growth, and ensures the next generation is prepared to lead and compete on a global scale. A nation that invests in its youngest learners isn't just preparing them for the future—it's securing its own.

The resistance was fierce, but so was the momentum. The data spoke louder than the critics. The voices of educators, parents, and policymakers who had seen dual-language success firsthand could no longer be ignored.

Then, on June 2, 2016, it happened. President Obama signed a historic policy reform enabling federal funding for dual-language early education. For the first time, millions of children would have access to curriculums that helped them learn English faster—giving them a stronger foundation for academic success and future careers. This wasn't just a policy win; it was a defining moment in early education, proving that systemic change was possible when vision, strategy, and collaboration aligned.

The recognition that followed was both humbling and deeply symbolic. General Ray Odierno, then Army Chief of Staff, honored me with his challenge coin—a rare distinction in military tradition, given only to those who have demonstrated extraordinary leadership and impact. As if that moment weren't surreal enough, he later arranged for me to tandem jump with the elite Army Golden Knights. Free falling from 12,500 feet, I felt the rush of adrenaline, but more than that, I felt the weight of what had been accomplished—the realization that bold action, persistence, and the right coalition of allies could drive change at the highest levels.

Then came a moment I never could have imagined. Standing in the White House, I listened as President Obama personally thanked me for my leadership. It was surreal—a testament to how far this journey had taken me. What began with a single effort to help a young girl read had grown into something far greater. It was proof that bold ideas, relentless persistence, and the right allies could create lasting change.

But more than anything, it reaffirmed a powerful truth: preparing people with the skills and education to compete on a global stage isn't just about individual achievement—it's about securing the future of a nation. Every step we had taken, every challenge we had faced, had led to this moment. And while the recognition was an honor, the true reward was knowing that the impact of our work would extend far beyond that day, shaping lives for generations to come.

It was proof that real change isn't made in a single sweeping moment but in the relentless pursuit of progress—the willingness to push forward when the path is uncertain, to stand firm when the obstacles seem insurmountable, and to believe, even when others doubt, that lasting impact is always possible for those who refuse to give up.

Back to the Future

And then came the call that would redefine everything—an invitation to lead one of the most iconic organizations in the nation as CEO of the Girl Scouts of the USA. This wasn't just another career move; it was a shift into something even greater.

Stepping into this role wasn't just about leading an organization—it was about preparing an entire generation of young women to lead with courage, confidence and character along with resilience, and purpose. The mission stretched far beyond any one initiative; it was about ensuring that girls everywhere had access to the skills and experiences that would allow them to shape their own futures.

It was a chance to take everything I had learned—about leadership, strategy, and breaking barriers—and apply it to an organization that had been equipping girls for over a century. But this time, it wasn't just about adapting to change—it was about leading it, ensuring the next generation had the skills, resilience, and vision to thrive in a world evolving faster than ever before.

9 | Building Trust

The stakes had never been higher. I was stepping into the leadership of one of the most storied organizations in the country—an institution that had shaped millions of lives, including my own. But this wasn't just about preserving a legacy; it was about reimagining the future. The Girl Scouts of the USA stood at a crossroads, facing challenges that required bold decisions and a vision for the future.

Everything I had learned—every risk taken, every barrier broken, every lesson forged in the fires of experience—had led to this moment. This wasn't just about leading an organization; it was about ensuring that the next generation of young women had the skills, confidence, and vision to lead in a world that was changing faster than ever before.

This chapter isn't just about stepping up—it's about stepping forward. It's about the kind of leadership that doesn't just respond to challenges but reshapes them into opportunities. It's about proving that with courage, conviction, and an unwavering commitment to impact, you don't just lead—you transform.

Girl Scouts of the USA

In 2008, I joined the national board of directors for Girl Scouts of the USA, a connection made possible by the legendary Governor Ann Richards. This wasn't just an honor—it was personal. The Girl Scouts had profoundly shaped my life, and serving on the board felt like a chance to give back to an organization that had given me so much.

When the previous CEO announced her departure in 2016, as a board member, I was asked to step in as interim CEO. For those who knew me well, this transition made perfect sense. My lifelong connection to the Girl Scouts and the values it instilled in me were well-known as I had written *Path to the Stars: My Journey from Girl Scout to Rocket Scientist*, a memoir written for middle school readers, which celebrated the organization's transformative role in my life. This new role wasn't just an opportunity; it felt like a calling—a chance to lead the Girl Scouts through a pivotal moment in its storied history.

A Test of Trust

Stepping into the role of interim CEO was anything but smooth. The transition was choppy—two former board members had already turned it down, and skepticism surrounded my appointment. To many in the Girl Scout community, I was just a board member filling a temporary gap, a placeholder rather than the bold leader they believed the organization needed in this critical moment.

What they didn't see was the full scope of my experience. They knew my background in education advocacy, but not the years I had spent in business—navigating complex transitions, driving strategy, and executing high-stakes turnarounds. Their doubt was clear, a constant reminder that trust would have to be earned, not assumed.

But I had spent my entire career proving people wrong, turning uncertainty into opportunity, and stepping into roles where the odds were stacked against me. This was no different. I wasn't just here to steady the ship—I was here to chart a new course.

The reaction to my appointment buzzed with uncertainty, and the skepticism was unmistakable. Trust wouldn't come from my title or any past accomplishments—it had to be earned. In any CEO transition, especially an unexpected one, doubt was inevitable. Words alone wouldn't be enough; empty assurances wouldn't quell concerns.

The only way forward was through action—thoughtful decisions, decisive leadership, and a willingness to face challenges head-on. I knew I had to prove, not just claim, that I was the right leader for this moment. The stakes were high, and success was far from guaranteed. But I was ready to rise to the challenge and show that my leadership would not only steady the organization but propel it forward.

Because You Are a Girl Scout

Stepping into the role of CEO felt like stepping onto the deck of a ship in the middle of a storm—intense, exhilarating, and you never knew when the boat was going to tip you over. This was more than a leadership challenge; it was an opportunity to redefine what the Girl Scouts could be in an era of unprecedented change.

The stakes had never been higher, and the clock was ticking. My action plan wasn't just a roadmap; it was a promise to guide the next generation of girls into leaders who would chart their own path in the world.

To do that required rallying the staff at GSUSA and the 111 independent councils, their CEOs, Boards, and staff all across the country. My first meeting was with GSUSA staff at the headquarters in New York City. I could sense their skepticism and hesitation, which didn't upset or surprise me. They didn't know me or my professional journey. During this first meeting, I chose not to communicate my vision or operational changes, but rather, what bound all of us. What it meant to be a Girl Scout.

I told them a story.

It was a story of an airport delay at JFK Airport. If anyone has flown out of JFK, you know, this isn't a unique story. Weather disruptions had grounded flights all evening, and our plane sat on the tarmac for hours, engines ready but going nowhere. By 1:00 a.m., the inevitable announcement came: the flight was canceled. At that point, options were grim, the storm was raging and we all made do with whatever scraps of comfort we could find: stiff chairs or cold concrete floors.

It was uncomfortable and annoying at best, but I felt for people with small children. Throughout the night, strangers approached me—mothers, fathers—asking the same thing: "Will you watch my child while I use the bathroom?" Each time, I said yes, cradling sleepy toddlers as their parents sought brief relief. By dawn, a man handed me his two children. I agreed but couldn't help asking, "Why me? You don't even know me."

He pointed to my bag which had a small Girl Scout logo on it and said, "Because you're a Girl Scout. I know I can trust you to keep my children safe, even if I don't know your name."

As I finished recounting this moment to the GSUSA staff, the room was silent, every eye fixed on me. I paused and said, "That's what the Girl Scouts mean to people. It's not just a name or a logo—it's trust, safety, integrity, and goodness. It's a promise of who we are. And as staff, we're not just doing a job; we're the living embodiment of that promise. The world is watching to see how we uphold it."

I scanned the room and continued, "I'm here to protect and elevate this legacy. I will give everything I have to this mission, but I can't do it alone. I need your commitment, your belief in what the Girl Scouts stand for. Together, we can honor our legacy and take it to even greater heights."

In 1912, Juliette Gordon Low founded GSUSA with a bold vision, declaring she had something for the girls of America. Now, it's our turn. This is our moment to ensure that Girl Scouts remains relevant, that we equip girls with the skills, confidence, and leadership they need to thrive in the 21st century. The world is evolving—so must we. It is our moment to show the nation what it truly means to be a Girl Scout in this new era.

Real Leadership vs. Titles

What I had learned throughout my career, across every industry and every role, was that leadership wasn't about waiting for the perfect moment or unanimous approval—it was about seizing opportunities and earning trust in real time. Key stakeholders emerge in every environment, and the moments with the greatest potential often come during times of disruption or uncertainty. These are the moments when leaders must step forward with clarity and conviction.

One of the biggest mistakes I've seen leaders make is to assume that their position or title earns the trust and respect of their staff. There is respect for a title, but the trust is hard-earned and doesn't happen overnight. It requires building strong connections with key staff and influencers, engaging core stakeholders, and demonstrating consistent actions backed by crystal-clear communication.

A leader must communicate a vision so compelling it moves people—*not just to follow, but to see their place within it.* When people see not only what they're working toward but why it matters, they don't just work harder—they work with heart.

Leadership is never about universal approval—it's about making the tough calls, even in the face of resistance. Change breeds skepticism, and a leader who waits for unanimous agreement before acting will never move forward. True leadership demands conviction—the ability to assess the landscape, trust your judgment, and make bold decisions, knowing that action, not consensus, is what drives progress.

I had learned these lessons not from theory but through experience, navigating high-stakes environments where hesitation meant falling behind. Now, as I stepped into this critical role, I knew these principles would be tested once again. But I also knew that trust is earned through courage, consistency, and results. And that's exactly what I was prepared to deliver.

Building Trust

Building trust wasn't theoretical—it was a relentless, boots-on-the-ground commitment. As CEO, I knew leadership couldn't be dictated from behind a desk in New York City. It had to be earned, face-to-face, by showing up, listening, and proving through action that I understood the weight of this mission. Having navigated the pitfalls of misalignment with leadership earlier in my career, I understood that trust wasn't automatic—it had to be built. And that started with the CEOs running local Girl Scout councils across the country.

My first year, I spent over 200 days on the road, an unprecedented level of engagement for a national CEO—a commitment I maintained until the COVID-19 pandemic forced travel to a halt. I didn't just visit councils; I immersed myself in their realities. This wasn't just a leadership tour—it was personal. I had grown up in a small rural town, where opportunity often felt like something that existed somewhere else, for someone else. But Girl

Scouts changed that for me. It gave me the skills, confidence, and leadership ability that would propel me far beyond the boundaries of my hometown. It taught me how to set ambitious goals, adapt in the face of challenges, and see possibilities where others only saw limitations.

Now, as I traveled across the country, I saw firsthand what I had once lived—the way Girl Scouts could open a world of opportunity for girls in rural communities, giving them their first glimpse of what was possible beyond their surroundings. I met girls who reminded me of myself at their age—curious, ambitious, and eager to discover what lay beyond the familiar. In those small towns, Girl Scouts wasn't just an after-school activity; it was a launchpad.

Then, in the heart of Silicon Valley, I walked into the boardrooms of some of the most powerful tech companies in the world. And what I found was striking. Many of the women who had risen to the highest levels of leadership in these companies shared something in common—they had been Girl Scouts. They credited the persistence, courage, and leadership skills they learned in those early years with helping them break barriers and carve out their paths in a male-dominated industry.

I knew firsthand how valuable those lessons were because I had lived them myself. In Silicon Valley, I had to push through doubt, navigate setbacks, and prove that I belonged. The same resilience and courage that had carried me from my small town to NASA and beyond were the very qualities I saw reflected in these women. The connection was undeniable: the skills that Girl Scouts instilled in young girls weren't just nice to have—they were foundational for future leaders.

And so, as I traveled from one end of the country to the other, I saw the full arc of what Girl Scouts could do. It wasn't just about badges or camping trips—it was about shaping leaders, unlocking potential, and ensuring that every girl, no matter where she started, had the tools to write her own future. Because whether in a rural town or in Silicon Valley, the ability to lead, persist, and thrive wasn't about where you came from—it was about what you had been prepared to do. And Girl Scouts had been doing exactly that for generations.

Every mile traveled reinforced a fundamental truth: leading an organization with the scale and legacy of Girl Scouts required more than making decisions from headquarters—it demanded deep understanding, adaptability, and a relentless commitment to ensuring every girl, no matter where she lived, had access to the skills and opportunities to thrive.

In the middle of America's industrial heartland, I stood before 3,000 women at a business convention. After a fireside chat, I was asked about any lasting benefits of Girl Scouts. Instead of delivering a speech filled with statistics or anecdotes, I chose something simpler—something that needed no explanation. I sang three familiar words: "Make new friends."

For a split second, there was silence. Then, like a wave rolling across the room, voices rose in unison. Women from every background, every industry, joined in, their voices filling the space with the song that had connected generations of Girl Scouts. Some laughed as they remembered the lyrics, others swayed, caught up in the nostalgia of a childhood lesson that had stayed with them.

That moment said more than any speech ever could. It was living proof of the Girl Scouts' enduring impact—not just in childhood, but across a lifetime. The bonds, the lessons, the confidence built within this organization didn't fade with time; they remained, shaping leaders, innovators, and changemakers long after their last troop meeting.

Everywhere I went, the connection was deeply personal and undeniably powerful. Meeting with Girl Scouts, I sang rounds of camp songs with young girls, reliving the same moments that had shaped my own childhood. With volunteers, I listened to their challenges, their ideas, and their unwavering dedication to shaping the next generation of leaders. I prioritized face-to-face conversations with local council CEOs and staff, knowing that trust wasn't built through memos or mandates—it was earned through presence, understanding, and shared commitment.

These weren't just symbolic gestures. Every visit, every conversation, every song sung in unison sent a clear and unwavering message: You matter. Your work matters. We are in this together. By showing up—not just in boardrooms, but in tiny towns, at campgrounds, in school gyms, and in packed convention halls—I was reinforcing the fabric of the Girl Scout community, ensuring that no girl or volunteer ever felt unseen or left behind.

Macaroni Necklaces and Cookies

Leading the Girl Scouts of the USA was a defining moment in my career—a chance to take a century-old institution, rich with tradition, and propel it into the future. The mission was clear: honor the legacy while evolving to meet the realities of a fast-moving, tech-driven world. The stakes? Nothing less than ensuring Girl Scouts remained as vital for the next generation as it had been for the millions who came before.

The turning point came not from boardroom discussions or data reports, but from listening—really listening—to the voices that mattered most. Girls, parents, troop leaders, and volunteers all echoed the same truth: nostalgia alone wouldn't sustain the movement. Girls wanted more. They craved experiences that were bold, relevant, and empowering—tools that would prepare them not just to participate in the future, but to lead it.

Then came a moment that cut through all the noise. A father, arms crossed, looked me straight in the eye and asked, "Why should my daughter join Girl Scouts? She's just going to make macaroni necklaces and sell cookies." His words landed like a challenge, encapsulating the skepticism we were up against.

That question wasn't just about his daughter. It was about every girl who had yet to see herself in the Girl Scouts, who needed to know this wasn't just an organization of the past—it was a launching pad for the future. And in that moment, I knew: We weren't just refreshing a brand or tweaking a curriculum. We were redefining what it meant to be a Girl Scout in the 21st century.

But evolution didn't mean abandoning tradition. It meant honoring the legacy while expanding its reach. One hand firmly held onto the best of what had made Girl Scouts a powerhouse of leadership—character-building, service, outdoor adventure—while the other reached forward, grasping the tools and skills today's girls needed to thrive in an increasingly complex world. It was about keeping the campfires burning while sparking new possibilities—offering badges in coding, cybersecurity, robotics, automotive, space, and other STEM fields that would equip girls with the skills to lead in the careers of tomorrow.

The Girl Scouts had always been about preparing girls for leadership. Now, it was time to ensure they were prepared for a future that was faster, more digital, and more demanding than ever before. The challenge wasn't just to modernize—it was to evolve with purpose, to prove that a movement founded in 1912 was just as vital, just as powerful, and just as necessary today as it was over a century ago.

Girls were already deeply immersed in digital technology—it shaped how they connected, communicated, and explored the world around them. The challenge wasn't just keeping pace with their engagement; it was equipping them to move beyond being consumers of technology to becoming its creators, innovators, and leaders. At the same time, the future workforce was demanding exactly these skills. This intersection of need and potential became the driving force behind my leadership vision.

Parents weren't looking for their daughters to just earn badges in camping or crafting—they wanted experiences that would expand their horizons, from coding and robotics to outdoor adventure and entrepreneurial leadership. This wasn't about leaving tradition behind—it was about building on its strongest foundations, ensuring that Girl Scouts remained not just relevant but essential in preparing girls for a world full of possibility.

This vision was a direct continuation of Juliette Gordon Low's legacy—a future-focused movement designed to prepare girls for what's next. She founded Girl Scouts at a pivotal moment in history, as the world shifted from an agrarian society to an industrial age. The first badges weren't just symbols; they were cutting-edge skills of the time—electricity, carpentry, and aviation—ensuring girls could step confidently into a rapidly evolving world.

Now, as the world transitioned from the industrial age to the digital era, the mission remained the same: equip girls with the tools to lead, innovate, and thrive. This wasn't a departure from tradition; it was a reaffirmation of it—honoring the essence of Girl Scouts by ensuring that each generation was prepared not just for the present, but for the future they would shape.

This vision didn't just resonate within the Girl Scouts—it captured the attention of some of the most influential leaders in business and technology. Companies like GM, Palo Alto Networks, Salesforce, and Raytheon understood that the demand for a digitally skilled workforce wasn't just a Silicon Valley issue—it was a national imperative. They saw in Girl Scouts a unique opportunity: the only national organization for girls with the scale, reach, and proven track record to deliver impactful programming in every residential zip code across America.

By aligning their commitment to workforce development with our mission to equip girls with modern leadership skills, we transformed an ambitious idea into a powerful movement. These partnerships weren't just about funding initiatives; they were about shaping the future—ensuring that girls across the country had access to the tools, training, and opportunities to step confidently into the careers of tomorrow.

At the Speed of Girl

Girls were already immersed in technology, but I saw an opportunity to take them further—not just as users, but as creators, inventors, and designers of technology. However, for this vision to succeed, the entire organization had to evolve and move "at the speed of girl."

When I stepped into the CEO role in 2016, only six new badges were in development, with some projected for release as late as 2025—far too slow in a world advancing at a rapid pace. We needed a fundamental shift. The teams in the Program Office and Girl Scout Research Institute (GSRI) embraced an agile development approach, cutting timelines dramatically. Instead of working in isolation, we formed strategic partnerships with leading organizations, tapping into their expertise while focusing on what Girl Scouts does best—creating hands-on, girl-centered learning experiences that foster leadership and confidence.

This shift didn't just accelerate progress; it ensured that every new badge was meaningful, relevant, and built to equip girls with the skills they needed to thrive in a fast-changing world.

As an example, to inspire seven- and eight-year-old Brownies to explore cybersecurity, we didn't start with abstract concepts—we met them where they were. What do young girls love? Talking to each other. So, we used that natural inclination to bring the world of networks and malware to life in a way they could grasp.

Sitting in a circle, the girls tossed a ball of yarn back and forth as they chatted, creating an intricate web of connections. Then came the twist: one girl was "infected" with a virus. Because they were all linked in the same "network," the virus quickly spread to everyone. In that moment, they didn't just hear about cybersecurity—they experienced it. They saw firsthand how networks function and how cyber threats spread. And more importantly, they learned that just like in the digital world, they had the power to protect themselves and others.

These early hands-on experiences didn't just introduce STEM concepts; they ignited curiosity, confidence, and competence. As the girls advanced through the badge programs, they tackled increasingly complex challenges, growing from understanding basic digital safety to exploring coding, encryption, and ethical hacking. Each new skill reinforced the belief that technology wasn't just something to use—it was something they could master and shape.

Rolling out these programs nationally required an ambitious vision and relentless execution. The Girl Scout council support team aligned an aggressive training timeline with the rapid development of new badge programs. The result? In under four years, we launched 146 new programs—126 of them STEM-focused—a historic transformation that redefined what Girl Scouts could offer. We also created badges for outdoor leadership. Partnering with The North Face, we expanded outdoor adventure programs, ensuring girls had the skills and confidence to explore the natural world. Our Entrepreneurship badges empowered girls to think like entrepreneurs, building financial literacy and business acumen through the real-world experiences of the cookie program. Meanwhile, our Civics badges reinforced the importance of civic engagement, educating girls on how our government works, why their voices matter, and how they can drive meaningful change.

This was more than just a badge expansion—it was a movement to equip girls with the skills, knowledge, and courage to shape their own futures. Whether they were learning to navigate the backcountry, pitch a business idea, or advocate for policy change, these programs reinforced one core message: leadership isn't just something you wait for—it's something you step up and create.

The impact was undeniable. Across the country, local councils saw an explosion of enthusiasm, with businesses eager to invest in girls' futures. New partnerships flourished in fields like automotive engineering, space, coding, robotics, cybersecurity, and design thinking. The badge programs became more than just activities—they became a gateway, connecting girls to the future workforce and their own limitless potential.

This wasn't just a modernization of Girl Scouts. It was a revolution—one that ensured that every girl, no matter where she lived, could see herself as a leader, an innovator, and a force for the future.

Core Belief

By my final full year as CEO, over one million STEM badges were being earned annually by girls across America—in rural towns, bustling cities, and everywhere in between. This wasn't just a number; it was a transformation. It was proof that when you give girls access to opportunity, they rise to meet it.

For me, this was deeply personal. As a young Girl Scout in a small rural town, earning a science badge wasn't just an activity—it was a spark. It ignited my curiosity, gave me the confidence to tackle challenges, and built the foundation in science and math that propelled me to a life of limitless potential. That single badge set me on a path to NASA, Silicon Valley, and beyond.

Now, across the country, girls were discovering their own sparks. They weren't just earning badges; they were gaining the skills, confidence, and vision to lead in the digital world. They were seeing themselves as engineers, coders, innovators, and problem-solvers—ready to shape the future, not just navigate it.

This was more than a program; it was a revolution in how we prepare girls to lead. It was a testament to bold ideas, decisive action, and the unwavering belief that every girl, no matter where she comes from, holds the power to redefine leadership and seize opportunities that once seemed out of reach.

The impact of our work extended far beyond the Girl Scout movement. When we announced the launch of our cybersecurity badges, it didn't just make headlines—it ignited a national conversation. While Girl Scouts had long been known for its iconic Cookie Program, this bold new initiative reintroduced the organization in a way that captured the urgency and excitement of the modern world.

The news spread like wildfire, generating over a billion media impressions and sparking discussions in households, classrooms, and boardrooms across America. Parents saw the future opening up for their daughters. Educators saw a new way to engage girls in STEM. Business leaders saw the next generation of talent being cultivated in real time.

This wasn't just about badges—it was about belief. A belief in every girl's ability to lead in the digital age, to innovate, to solve complex problems, and to step into careers once thought beyond reach. It was also a powerful reminder that Girl Scouts wasn't just keeping up with the times—it was shaping the future.

Leg Up in Life

That day in Wichita, Kansas, amidst the biting cold and the remnants of an ice storm, I was reminded why this work mattered in ways no statistic or media headline ever could. The event, a hands-on Girl Scout STEM experience, had already exceeded my expectations. Despite the treacherous weather, more than 100 girls and their families had made the journey, their determination evident in every excited voice and eager pair of hands working on a coding activity, a leadership challenge, or assembling and programming robots.

As I saw a mother and father watching their daughter, I struck up a conversation asking them if they lived nearby. The mother gestured toward her husband and said, "He drove four hours through the ice storm so we could be here." Concerned, I turned to him and said, "Sir, I admire your resolve, but Girl Scouts is always about safety." He gave me a knowing smile and said, "You don't know much about Kansas, do you?" I admitted that I didn't. Then he looked me squarely in the eye and said something I'll never forget:

"Our heyday was during and right after World War II. We had factories, good jobs, and a path forward for our kids. But those jobs are gone now, and we're losing too many of our young people—to dead-end futures and to addiction. What our daughter is learning here—STEM skills, leadership, confidence—this gives her a leg up in life. It would be far more dangerous for us to stay home and let her miss this opportunity."

His words were a gut punch, a truth so stark and undeniable that it made everything else fade away. This wasn't just about a STEM event. It wasn't just about Girl Scouts. It was about something much deeper—the fundamental promise of opportunity.

That father's determination embodied what Girl Scouts truly stood for: the belief that no girl, no matter where she was born or what obstacles stood in her way, should be denied the chance to reach her full potential. This was why we pushed forward, why we fought to modernize, why we expanded our programs. It was never just about badges or initiatives—it was about ensuring that every girl had access to the tools that could change her life.

I walked away from that conversation with a renewed sense of purpose. This was the legacy we were building. Not one measured by numbers alone, but by the futures we helped shape, by the doors we helped open, and by the families—like that one in Kansas—who refused to let anything stand in the way of their daughter's future.

Evolving a Movement

Leading a 100-plus-year-old institution like the Girl Scouts of the USA felt like standing at the intersection of history and possibility. It wasn't just about steering an organization—it was about safeguarding a legacy, a movement that had shaped generations of girls while carrying the hopes and dreams of millions more.

As a leader, you inherit what you inherit: triumphs that inspire, traditions that anchor, challenges that test, and complexities that demand clarity. But with that inheritance comes a profound responsibility—a duty to not merely preserve what is but to shape what could be, ensuring the institution stands stronger and is more relevant for those who come next.

Through teamwork, storytelling, and bold innovation, we modernized the Girl Scouts while preserving its century-old legacy. The organization moved forward faster, staying true to its mission while adapting to a changing world. With a renewed sense of purpose, it became stronger and more unified.

But as we celebrated these strides, we unknowingly stood on the edge of an unprecedented challenge. It wasn't just the girls we had prepared to thrive in a digital age; we had also readied the entire organization to be agile and fully digital—a transformation that was about to face an ultimate test. What lay ahead would demand everything from us and more, reminding us that progress, no matter how inspiring, is never without its trials.

The Rose Bowl Float, the Dawn Before the Storm

Standing on a float in the iconic New Year's Day parade in Pasadena, California, waving to a sea of spectators, I felt the weight of history beneath my feet. It was an honor to represent the Girl Scouts alongside Gold Award Girl Scout Genetha Cleveland and the legendary Girl Scout alum Dolores Huerta as well as many other women leaders on a float commemorating the passage of the 19th Amendment. The moment was deeply personal for Girl Scouts, an organization founded in 1912—eight years before women had the right to vote. From the beginning, Girl Scouts instilled the power of civic engagement, launching the Citizens Badge in 1920 to encourage young women to play a role in shaping the fast-changing world around them. In the first elections after the passage of the 19th Amendment, Girl Scouts played a vital role, caring for children barred from polling places so their mothers could cast their ballots. It wasn't just service—it was action, a reminder that progress isn't only won in protests and speeches, but in the determined, everyday efforts that make participation possible.

That day, as I waved to the cheering crowds, I felt immense pride in representing a movement far bigger than myself. The float wasn't just a celebration—it was a tribute to generations of Girl Scouts who had quietly shaped history. Under the bright Pasadena sun, the moment was filled with promise, a symbol of the progress made and the possibilities still ahead.

COVID-19

Then, just weeks later, the distant whispers of COVID-19 exploded into a global crisis, thrusting the Girl Scouts into uncharted territory, where every decision carried unprecedented stakes. Safety—a fundamental pillar of our organization—became the driving force behind every decision. What started with hand sanitizers at headquarters and enhanced cleaning protocols quickly escalated as New York City became the national epicenter of the pandemic.

Overnight, everything changed. A carefully phased rollout of remote technology was no longer a long-term strategy—it became an immediate, all-hands-on-deck effort to keep the organization running in a world that had suddenly shut down. Across every level, from national headquarters to local councils, the Girl Scout movement mobilized, adapting with remarkable speed and resilience.

200-Hour Pivot

The heart of Girl Scouting—troop meetings, cookie booths, and outdoor adventures—was suddenly upended. The pandemic struck at the worst possible time: right in the middle of Girl Scout cookie season. Councils across the country were in vastly different stages of their sales—some had already finished, others had barely begun. For many, cookie revenue wasn't just a tradition; it was the financial lifeline that funded programs, camps, and community initiatives.

With conflicting information and mounting risks, I made the toughest call of my tenure: to cancel all in-person cookie sales. It was a decision that carried massive consequences, but safety had to come first. The weight of it was immense—I knew that the responsibility for the organization, for the girls, their families, and the councils, rested squarely on my shoulders.

We needed a bold pivot, not just to survive the crisis but to emerge stronger. I announced two unprecedented moves—initiatives that, just a few years earlier, would have been dismissed as impossible. First, we would transition all badge programming to digital platforms, ensuring that girls could continue learning, growing, and connecting, no matter the shutdowns. Second, for the first time in Girl Scout history, we would launch a onetime national online cookie sales platform, providing a critical revenue stream for councils hit hardest by the pandemic. And we wouldn't take months to roll this out—we gave ourselves two weeks.

This wasn't just about reacting to a crisis; it was a testament to the movement we had become. The rollout of 146 new badges had already proven that Girl Scouts was no slow-moving institution—we were an organization fueled by innovation, agility, and a deep commitment to meeting the needs of girls in real time. Now, we were putting that adaptability to the ultimate test.

What followed was a mobilization like no other. Headquarters staff, council CEOs, volunteers, and teams across the country worked around the clock, logging back-to-back 100-hour weeks. It was an all-hands effort, driven by a shared, unwavering commitment: to ensure that every girl, in every community, could stay engaged, supported, and connected.

This was more than a crisis response—it was a defining moment. It showed the world what Girl Scouts truly stood for: resilience, ingenuity, and an unshakable dedication to its mission. A 100-year-old organization didn't just weather the storm—it proved it could move at the speed of purpose, setting the stage for a new generation of leadership.

Determined to stay connected, I took daily walks through my neighborhood, phone in hand, speaking with council CEOs to navigate the challenges together. By the end of three months, I had already worn through a pair of sneakers and started on my second—a small but fitting symbol of the relentless effort it took to keep the movement moving forward. This wasn't just leadership; it was a full-body commitment to ensuring that Girl Scouts didn't just survive but thrive.

A Testament to Resilience

The results spoke volumes about the resilience and determination of the entire Girl Scout movement. In the darkest days of the pandemic, when over 600 lives were being lost daily in Manhattan, not a single member of our NYC headquarters staff succumbed to COVID-19, and no Girl Scout contracted the virus through Girl Scout activities during those critical months. These weren't just statistics—they were proof of what happens when an organization moves with clarity, purpose, and an unshakable commitment to safety and adaptability.

But the true measure of resilience wasn't in the numbers—it was in the girls themselves. Across the country, Girl Scouts stepped up in extraordinary ways. They fired up 3D printers to create face shields for frontline workers, hand-sewed tens of thousands of masks to protect their communities, and led service projects to support those most in need. When the world felt uncertain, they responded with action. These weren't just acts of kindness; they were demonstrations of courage, leadership, and the enduring power of the Girl Scout spirit.

The pandemic didn't stop these girls—it proved what they were capable of. It was a moment that reaffirmed everything the organization stood for: resilience in the face of adversity, innovation in times of crisis, and the unwavering belief that when girls lead, they make the world a better place.

Stewardship of a Legacy

Leadership in an institution like the Girl Scouts demands profound humility. You step into a role that is temporary, knowing you are entrusted with a legacy that is eternal. You may not solve every challenge or fulfill every ambition, but you can strive to guide the organization toward something greater. During my time as CEO, I embraced my role as a steward—honoring its storied past, fortifying its present, and laying a foundation for a brighter future.

For me, leadership was never about personal achievement—it was about stewardship. My guiding principle was simple yet profound: leave the campground better than you found it. Every decision, every initiative, and every challenge was met with one fundamental question: "Am I leaving this organization stronger, more relevant, and better prepared to serve future generations?"

That responsibility wasn't a burden—it was an honor. Leadership isn't about power or titles; it's about service. It's about carrying forward a mission greater than yourself, one built not just for the present, but for the future. And when done right, leadership ensures that long after you've left, the impact of your work continues to shape lives.

Journey's End, Echoes Endure

Every three years, Girl Scouts from across the nation gather for a convention—a pivotal gathering where critical decisions are made, including the election of the national board. It is a time of reflection, renewal, and transition. This particular convention also marked a turning point for the organization. A new board chair was set to take the reins, eager to lead Girl Scouts. With that change, I felt a deep sense of clarity: my own moment of transition had arrived.

Knowing when to step away is as vital as knowing when to step up. This wasn't an ending—it was the culmination of 12 years of national service, including four as CEO and eight as a national board member. Over those years, I had given everything I had to this movement, crisscrossing the country to meet with girls, volunteers, and council leaders. I had witnessed firsthand the profound impact of Girl Scouting in the lives of girls from all walks of life—those in big cities brimming with opportunity and those in small rural communities where possibilities seemed scarce. It had been grueling and demanding, but it was also the honor of a lifetime.

As I reflected on all we had accomplished together, I felt a deep sense of gratitude. It had been a privilege to work alongside an extraordinary staff at GSUSA and the dedicated council leaders across the nation. I had met volunteers—women and men—who weren't just supporters of Girl Scouts but true stewards of its mission. Their unwavering belief in the power of this organization had strengthened my own resolve every step of the way. Together, we had modernized programming, ensuring that girls weren't just learning skills for today but for the future. We had strengthened the cookie program, expanded the donor base, and made Girl Scouts more relevant than ever. But most importantly, we had invested in the next generation of leaders, giving them the confidence and tools to shape their own destinies. I felt joy and gratitude for the journey and a deep sense of peace knowing I had played my part.

A Legacy of Leadership

As I close this chapter, I am struck by a profound truth: *leadership is not about holding power—it's about unlocking potential.* It's about taking what you've been entrusted with, honoring its legacy, and daring to push it forward.

I am reminded of a moment that perfectly encapsulated the impact and legacy of this work. After delivering a speech in Birmingham, Alabama, I was approached by two families who had driven for hours from their rural community just to meet me and to share their story. Their daughters, Girl Scouts who had earned every cybersecurity badge, had written their college essays about how the program had changed their lives. Those essays earned them full-ride college scholarships—an opportunity that, for these families, had once felt unimaginable. In their rural hometown, where opportunities were scarce, Girl Scouts had provided a pathway to futures these families had only dreamed of. Standing before me, their parents spoke with tears in their eyes, sharing how Girl Scouts had opened doors they never thought possible for their daughters. Seeing the pride in their parents' eyes and hearing the hope in their voices was a moment I will never forget.

That moment cemented what I had always known: leadership in the Girl Scouts was never about me—it was about them. It was about the girls who found their voices, unlocked their strength, and built a future on a foundation we had helped lay. It was about ensuring that no matter where a girl came from, she had the chance to dream bigger, reach further, and step into her full potential. It was about creating a foundation strong enough to hold their ambitions and resilient enough to carry them into a future they would define.

Leadership is about taking what you've been entrusted with, honoring its legacy, and daring to push it forward. The Girl Scouts taught me that when you invest in potential, when you dare to reimagine what's possible, you don't just change lives—you shape the future. And that is a legacy worth the sacrifices and commitment.

10

The Door Opens from the Inside

This book isn't just a roadmap for success—it's a reflection on the moments that shaped me, the moments that nearly broke me, and the lessons that ultimately defined me. At the time, many of these setbacks felt unbearably crushing, but in hindsight, they were turning points. With resilience, the right support, and an unshakable determination to keep moving forward, they became the moments that mattered most.

Early in my career, I believed ambition was a solitary pursuit—a relentless climb to prove my worth over and over again. I built armor to shield myself from doubt, rejection, and the pain of my past. But that same armor, meant to protect me, also kept me isolated. What I didn't realize was that true success isn't about brute strength or individual resilience—it's about relationships. It's about working with others, trusting them, and understanding that leadership isn't about standing alone at the top, but about the people you bring with you along the way.

This final chapter isn't about reaching the summit—it's about what happens when you get there. And here's the irony: when the moment finally came, it wasn't a struggle, a battle, or a test. The doors opened because I had done the work—not just in my career, but in myself. I had learned to build trust, to lead with purpose, and to understand that real power doesn't come from proving yourself—it comes from knowing you belong.

Growth is uncomfortable. It challenges everything you thought you knew. But it's also where transformation happens. The lessons I've included in *The Trailblazer's Playbook* aren't just about leadership; they're about life. They're about the strength found in connection, the courage in vulnerability and seeking help when you need it, and the undeniable power of building something greater than yourself. Ultimately, success is not just measured by what you achieve, but also by the lasting impact you have and the future you inspire others to create.

Chutes and Ladders

Early in my career, as an engineer at IBM, I had the privilege of witnessing C-suite executives tour a state-of-the-art manufacturing facility that showcased design innovations I had contributed to. In that moment, I felt a longing and a desire—I wanted to be one of them. I didn't yet fully understand what that meant, but I knew I wanted to lead at the highest levels, to be part of shaping the future rather than just executing someone else's vision. At the time, IBM was the pinnacle of global leadership and innovation, and I set my sights on reaching the C-suite, believing success was a path in a straight line to the top.

But the truth is, the path to leadership is rarely linear. The greatest achievements don't always come from following a perfectly planned route, but from learning to navigate the unexpected—the roadblocks, the detours, the moments when the path forward disappears and you have to carve a new one.

What I've learned is that real leadership isn't just about reaching a title. It's about resilience in the face of uncertainty, about adapting to change, and about recognizing that sometimes, the most meaningful successes come from the challenges we never saw coming. The road may not look the way you envisioned, but if you stay open to growth, embrace the twists, and lead with purpose, you may find yourself somewhere even greater than you ever imagined.

This journey of mine has been one of transformation, resilience, and hope—a testament to the truth that the dreams we chase aren't just destinations, but paths that shape us in ways we never anticipated. Every challenge, every triumph, every failure has played a role in making me the leader I am today—not because I followed a perfect plan, but because I embraced the lessons, difficult as they were, hidden in the struggle.

To anyone reading this, know that your journey will be uniquely yours. Pursue your dreams with conviction, even when doubt creeps in, even when the obstacles feel insurmountable. Trust and develop your talent, lean into your resilience, and don't shy away from the hard moments—they shape you in ways success alone never could. Because in the end, success isn't just about reaching the top—it's about who you become along the way.

For most of my career, I believed that relentless drive and results were enough. And in many ways, they were. My ability to deliver results opened doors, moved me across industries, and led me to opportunities I had never imagined. But despite my achievements, one glaring truth remained: I wasn't being elevated within the organizations I served. I could perform at the highest level, but I wasn't seen as the person to take that next step in the organization.

At first, I rationalized it—blaming politics, biases, and being overlooked. But deep down, I had to face something even harder: the common denominator in every single situation was me. I had been so focused on proving myself that I failed to see the power of alignment, of building relationships with those who could help me grow. Authority figures weren't just obstacles to overcome—they were potential allies, mentors, and champions who could open doors I couldn't force open on my own. That realization changed everything.

It wasn't just about ambition—it was about connection. *Leadership isn't a solitary pursuit*; it's built through relationships, shared vision, and mutual trust. And in the process, I learned that growth isn't about going it alone—it's about surrounding yourself with those who recognize your potential, push you beyond your comfort zone, and challenge you in ways that force you to rise.

Looking back, I see what I couldn't always recognize in the moment—the profound impact of mentorship and sponsorship, even when I felt unseen or overlooked. Just as my parents' love had always been there, even when grief clouded my ability to feel it, the guidance and belief of others in authority had quietly shaped my path in ways I hadn't fully realized.

At IBM, when I was drowning in sorrow after losing my parents, my boss did something extraordinary—he gave me space, understanding, and support at a time when mental health was rarely acknowledged in the workplace. At Apple, a mentor saw beyond my role and pushed me into the world of global business, bringing me into high-level meetings where I absorbed the nuances of international leadership—an opportunity rarely extended to women at the time. At Dell, a senior VP gave me some of the hardest but most valuable feedback of my career—he didn't just acknowledge my results, he demanded that I articulate my impact with clarity and conviction. And then there was Ann Richards, the legendary Texas governor who embodied fearless leadership. She didn't just see my potential—she acted on it. With a single handwritten note to the Girl Scouts' board, she set me on the path to becoming its CEO, proving that true sponsorship isn't just about encouragement—it's about taking action that can change the entire trajectory of a career.

These moments weren't always obvious, and at times, I felt like I was alone on my professional journey. But now, I see the truth: No one succeeds in isolation. Every opportunity, every breakthrough, every step forward is shaped by those who see something in us before we see it in ourselves.

These moments, and so many others, taught me a truth that took me years to fully grasp: success is never a solo act. It's built through the hands of those who believe in you, push you, and open doors when you don't yet have the key. And as much as I've been shaped by those who supported me, I've also learned that the greatest measure of leadership isn't just how far you go—it's how many others you bring along with you.

And you never know who is watching you.

When we launched the Girl Scouts' cybersecurity badges, we weren't just rolling out a new program—we were igniting a movement. With the backing of key partners like Palo Alto Networks and Raytheon, what started as an idea became a force for change.

At Palo Alto Networks, Mark McLaughlin—then the former CEO and at the time the Board Chair—saw the vision take shape, the execution unfold, and the undeniable impact ripple outward. He stood beside me as we met with members of Congress, not in just any room, but in the office of then-Majority Leader Kevin McCarthy, high above Capitol Hill—a place where decisions that shape the nation are made.

In that moment, we weren't just advocating for a program; we were defining the future. A future where young girls wouldn't just consume technology but defend it. Where they would stand on the front lines of cybersecurity, protecting digital infrastructure and national security.

This wasn't just about badges. It was about building a pipeline of talent, strengthening America's workforce, and ensuring our leadership on the global stage. Because when you empower the next generation with the right skills, you don't just prepare them for the future—you help shape it.

Years later, after Mark became the Board Chair of Qualcomm, he called with an opportunity that carried a different weight. He had seen my leadership up close—not just in the boardrooms of Washington, but in the way I had turned vision into action. When I announced my departure as CEO of the Girl Scouts, Mark called to gauge my interest in joining the Qualcomm board. With CEO Cristiano Amon driving the company's transformation in AI, 5G, and the intelligent edge, it was a strong fit for my technology background and Qualcomm's strategic direction.

It was a full-circle moment—one that stretched all the way back to that young engineer at IBM, standing in awe of the IBM C-Suite executives. Back then, I had looked at those C-suite executives with admiration, knowing I wanted to be among them, even if I didn't yet fully understand what that meant. Now, after decades of leading, navigating challenges, and proving my value at the highest levels, I wasn't just being invited in the room—I had a seat at the table. I had gone from being the engineer who once aspired to leadership to serving on the board of a major technology company, being part of shaping the future of an industry that had defined so much of my career.

And then, another door opened—one I hadn't planned for but was more than ready to walk through.

A call came—an invitation to join the board of Dynamic Signal, a rising startup in the communications space. The connection? Eric Brown, the CEO who was a friend from Austin. We had reconnected at a Salesforce Dreamforce event, where Eric watched my main stage presentation. He saw the vision, the execution, the impact of what I had led at Girl Scouts.

Now, as CEO of Dynamic Signal, Eric was looking for an independent board member—someone who understood leadership, strategy, and how to scale with purpose. He had been watching. And when the moment came, he knew exactly who to call. As I began networking with other corporate board directors, another call came—this time from Credo Technologies, a company at the cutting edge of connectivity and innovation led by CEO Bill Brennon and Board Chair Lip-Bu Tan. The pattern was undeniable. These weren't random moments or lucky breaks. They were the result of years of showing up, cultivating a network, delivering results, and earning trust—not just through performance, but through the integrity and impact of my leadership.

When the time came, it didn't feel like a climb or a struggle anymore. The doors opened naturally—not because I demanded entry, but because my actions, experience, reputation, and the relationships I had built over the years had already spoken for me. These moments were a powerful reminder that when you lead with purpose, integrity, and an unwavering commitment to excellence, the world doesn't just open its doors. It invites you in.

Board Director

When I first set my sights on the C-suite, I didn't fully grasp what it meant to serve on a board of directors. I had spent my career leading from an operational and tactical lens, driving execution and results. But board leadership demanded something different—a higher-level perspective of governance, strategy, risk management, and long-term viability. It wasn't just about steering a company forward; it was about safeguarding its future.

When I entered the boardroom of a publicly traded company, I quickly realized that having a seat at the table came with a profound responsibility. It wasn't enough to bring expertise in leadership and strategy—I had to think like a corporate steward, ensuring that bold innovation was balanced with sound oversight, and that immediate business success aligned with long-term sustainability. The shift from executive to board member was not just a transition in role, but in mindset.

Governance became one of the most fascinating and challenging aspects of my board service. I had spent my career making decisions and driving change, but in the boardroom, the role was different. It wasn't about your operational excellence; instead, it is about ensuring that the right leaders, systems, and safeguards are in place to keep the company successful for the long term and to drive shareholder value. Governance wasn't just about policies and procedures; it was about setting the tone at the top, ensuring transparency, and maintaining trust with shareholders, employees, and the broader community.

I quickly realized that effective board leadership isn't just about oversight—it's about leveraging experience, strategic acumen, and collaboration to guide a company through both opportunities and uncertainties. The topics that land on a board's agenda aren't just theoretical—they have real-world consequences that shape the company's future.

Take the concept of risk management as an example. It's not just about reacting to crises; it's about seeing around corners, identifying potential vulnerabilities before they become existential threats, and putting the right safeguards in place to keep the company resilient. Whether it's cybersecurity threats, regulatory changes, or supply chain disruptions, the board plays a crucial role in ensuring the company is not just prepared for the unexpected but positioned to thrive despite it.

Ultimately, a strong board isn't just a safeguard—it's a strategic force that challenges leadership to think ahead, take smart risks, and create lasting value. The best boards don't just provide oversight of a company's business; they push it toward a stronger future.

Strong governance isn't about avoiding risk; it's about ensuring the right risks are taken with discipline and foresight. True innovation and transformation require a foundation of accountability and strategic vision.

A great board operates like a highly skilled team, where each member brings expertise, stays sharp on industry and geopolitical shifts, and contributes at the highest level. Board meetings aren't about speaking just to be heard—they're about knowing when to listen and when to offer insight that moves the conversation forward. The real impact comes not from dominating discussions, but from asking the right questions, offering perspective, and ensuring the company is positioned for both opportunity and resilience. The best boards don't just oversee—they elevate, challenging leadership to think bigger while holding them accountable to execute with precision.

Serving on corporate boards has been one of the most dynamic and rewarding chapters of my career. It has placed me at the forefront of geopolitical changes, supply chain disruptions, and the rapid evolution of AI—forces that are redefining industries in real time. But more than offering a front-row seat to change, it has reinforced a deeper truth: leadership isn't just about driving transformation; it's about anticipating it, navigating complexity, and ensuring that the future isn't just different, but stronger, smarter, and more resilient than the past.

I've seen an extraordinary commitment from semiconductor and business executives who recognize that leadership development isn't optional—it's essential. Through the Global Semiconductor Alliance, I've partnered with the GSA CEO Jodi Shelton and other leaders who are dedicating their expertise and resources to accelerating executive talent development, including women, to ensure a strong and expanding leadership pipeline. This investment is critical, as semiconductors are not just at the core of AI but also power nearly every aspect of modern life, from healthcare to global infrastructure. The leaders we develop today will shape the future, driving innovation and reinforcing the semiconductor industry's role as the backbone of the global economy.

Gratitude

For every aspiring leader who sees their own ambition reflected in my story, know this: leadership isn't given—it's earned. It's not reserved for a select few; it belongs to those with vision, resilience, and the ability to create meaningful impact where it matters most. Opportunities don't simply appear; they come to those who consistently add value, think strategically, and solve real problems.

Leadership is also about gratitude—acknowledging those who paved the way before us. I may have been the first through many doors, but that was only possible because of the efforts of countless others who worked to make sure that there were doors to be opened. Leaders like Dr. Howard Adams of GEM, the program that provided the financial support that allowed me to attend Stanford. He played a crucial role in shaping my journey. Contributions like that of Dr. Adams remind us that no success is achieved alone—it's built on the foundation of those who came before us.

Because true leadership isn't just about earning a seat at the table—it's about keeping the door open for those who come next. It's about proving, through unwavering action and integrity, that success isn't measured by titles, but by the legacy you build and the lives you uplift.

It's a testament to resilience—to refusing to accept the story handed to you and instead writing your own. Adversity doesn't have to be a barrier; it can be the fire that forges you, the force that propels you beyond what anyone imagined possible.

But this journey was never just about me. It wasn't just a personal victory or the realization of a dream—it was something far greater. The impact rippled outward, transforming not only my life but my family's, my community's, and the countless others who saw in my story the proof that they, too, could rise.

Restoring Honor

When I stepped into the spotlight—as a CEO, a corporate board member, and a speaker sharing my story with the world—the recognition wasn't just about me. Every accolade, every milestone, was a symbol of resilience, a testament to redemption.

Then came a moment I will never forget. After appearing on a major network news show, my older brother sent me a message that took my breath away and brought tears to my eyes.

Mario wrote that after our parents' sudden deaths, a heavy shadow had fallen over our family, one we had each carried in different ways. That loss had left wounds, some visible, others buried. But through my journey, through every step I had taken to rise, I had done something more than just succeed. I had *restored dignity and honor* to our family name.

He told me that I had bent the arc of our family's history—away from grief and loss, toward something good, something lasting. And that through my perseverance, I had given our family a legacy not of tragedy, but of triumph.

I held his words in my hands, feeling their weight. In that moment, I understood with absolute clarity: this journey was never just mine. It was for my parents, who had dreamed bigger for their children than they had ever dared to dream for themselves. It was for my siblings and for every young person who had ever felt that their circumstances defined their limits. It was proof that no matter where you begin, no matter what heartbreaks you endure, you can rewrite your story. You can take pain and forge it into something powerful. You can rise, not just for yourself, but for everyone who never got the chance to.

That realization—that our journeys can ripple far beyond what we see—will stay with me forever. The journey is about who you lift, who you heal, and the hope you ignite in others along the way.

Passing the Baton

The lesson is clear—success isn't a straight path, nor is it defined by flawless execution. It is shaped by resilience, by purpose, and by the willingness to embrace the unexpected. I once believed that independence and defiance were my greatest strengths, but over time, I learned that true leadership isn't about standing alone—it's about standing together. It's about collaboration, shared vision, and the responsibility to lift others as you rise.

That's why I wrote this book. In my work on corporate boards and in speaking engagements across the world, I'm often asked the same question: How did you do it?

This book is my answer. It's not just a playbook for success—it's a baton, passed to the rising generation. It is a guide filled with real-world lessons, hard-won wisdom, and the vulnerabilities that shaped my journey. It is my message to anyone who has ever faced doubt or setbacks: these moments don't define the end of possibility. They are the beginning of something greater.

This chapter is both an acknowledgment and a heartfelt thank you—to the bosses who recognized my potential, the mentors and sponsors who opened doors, and the colleagues and friends who pushed, challenged, and supported me along the way.

And perhaps, in some ways, it is also an apology. I wasn't always the easiest person to guide. My drive was relentless, but at times, so was my defiance. My talent was evident, but my need to prove myself sometimes blinded me to the bigger picture. For those moments, I am sorry. But more than anything, I am profoundly grateful—for the patience, the belief, and the unwavering support that shaped the leader I ultimately became.

Lighting the Way Forward

This journey wasn't easy. It required every ounce of perseverance, courage, and belief in something bigger than myself. But it was worth it. Because when you rise from hardship, when you learn to forgive yourself and others, and when you lead with purpose, you don't just change your own story—you change the lives of others.

The Trailblazer's Playbook is my way of lighting the path forward, of passing on what I've learned so that others can take it further. And as I close this book, I do so with hope—hope for the rising leaders of tomorrow, hope for those who will take the Playbook baton and run even farther than I ever could.

Each time I step onto a stage, I see the faces of those who will shape the future—young leaders from all over the world ready to leave their own mark. I remind them that their talent, their drive, and their vision matter.

That the obstacles they face are not roadblocks but proving grounds. That their story, no matter where it begins, has the power to inspire, to break barriers, and to redefine what is possible.

Because that is the mission of a true trailblazer—not just to climb, but to turn struggle into strength, hope into action, and to leave behind a legacy that dares others to dream bigger, reach higher, and know, without a doubt, that they too can change the world.

Acknowledgments

Writing *The Trailblazer's Playbook* challenged me to revisit the most pivotal—and painful—chapters of my life. In doing so, I discovered that leadership isn't just about drive or results. It's also about forgiveness—for those who hurt us, for ourselves—and cultivating gratitude even amid loss. These are not soft ideas; they are strategic ones. They clear the path for clarity, courage, and conviction to lead.

I wrote this book because I know the profound weight of experiencing one of life's harshest tragedies and to feel you might not come back from it. But you can. You can recover. You can rebuild. Even when everything feels broken, even when you think you've lost too much, there is still a way forward.

But you can't do it alone. You need people who show up, who hold you up when you falter, who remind you why you started in the first place. Real friends. The kind who sit with you over endless cups of tea when you need to talk it through, who stand beside you in the quiet, heavy moments when you are not your best, who show up in the early mornings and stay through the long days.

I want you to know—you are not done. You are not defeated. You can rise again. And when you do, you'll see that the people who walked with you through the fire are the ones who made the victory possible.

To Those Who Never Let Me Go

I am profoundly grateful to my friends—the ones who stood beside me when everything was uncertain, when I was at my lowest, when it felt like my grief would never end. **You never let me go.** You didn't just offer encouragement; you carried some of the weight. Connie Nelson, Joy Hymel, Tina Chang, José Iglesias, Liz Meyerhoff, Julie Anderson, and Paula Kotzen—thank you. You reminded me who I was when I started to forget.

I am deeply grateful to the two therapists whose expertise and compassion guided me through my darkest moments. They taught me that seeking professional help isn't weakness but profound courage.

To my family, we endured something so painful, we each had to go our own way to find our way back, while never losing sight of the importance of family: Angelica Monge, Mario Acevedo, Armando Acevedo, Marina Galindo, Manaces Arteaga, Josue Arteaga, Marilu Pittman, and Cathy Barba. Through it all, we never lost one another.

To those who joined me in the work of improving educational outcomes for the rising generation—not because it was easy, but because it was worth it—thank you. Dr. Pat Forgione, Doyle Valdez, Kathrin Brewer, Nora Comstock, Susan Dawson, Jeanne Goka, Fely Garcia Amador, Marisa Limón Garza, Maelia Macin Davis, Luis Patino, Jorge Haynes, Toby Bushee, and Dr. Millie Garcia—your dedication changed lives. And to Christin Alvarado and Carissa Stengel—you were warriors in this battle, standing shoulder to shoulder when the odds seemed impossible. It couldn't have happened without you two. Thank you.

Thank you to the key players on the White House Commission to ensure the passage of federal policy to improve English language outcomes for Pre-K students, Dr. Eduardo Padrón, Dr. Linda Smith, Dr. Patricia Gándara, Nancy Navarro, Adrian Pedroza, Manny Sanchez, and Modesto Abety.

At Girl Scouts of the USA, we accomplished so much. Annette Freytag, Julie Golden, Judith Tanini, Lynelle McKay, Amy Bodin, and Savita Raj—looking back at the leadership to drive the work we did, you never lost sight

Acknowledgments

of the importance of making Girl Scouts relevant to girls and their parents. With over 146 new badges earned by millions of Girl Scouts, they've gained skills that give them an edge—for life. Thanks to all those at GSUSA who stepped up to the increased pace of transformation and delivered programs and services at an unprecedented speed. Girl Scouts is truly local; I am grateful to the CEOs and in particular to the council leaders who never hesitated to give me feedback, Lise Luttgens, Lidia Soto-Harmon, Marina Park, Mary Vitek, Tammy Wharton, Jennifer Bartkowski, Mary Anne Servian, Brian Newberry, Russel Statham, Carol Dedrich, Beth Shelton, and Karen Peterlin. Together, we never wavered in keeping the focus on the Girl in Girl Scouts. Dianne Belk, thank you for your generosity and amplifying legacy giving in Girl Scouts.

And my deepest thanks go to the volunteers and the Girl Scouts themselves. Seeing firsthand how Girl Scouts changed lives was always rejuvenating. I am in awe of the effort, commitment, and support of volunteers who make Girl Scouts come alive for girls in urban, suburban, and rural communities.

And to the friends who stand with me now, through all of life's seasons—with the grace of time and the wisdom we've earned—thank you. Kevin Finnegan, Eileen Finnegan, Helene Butler, Suzie Morris, Jan Hopkins, Hector Saldaña, Jill Ford, Kathy Reynolds, Lary Evans, Silvia Meyer, Sharon Moore, Sherry Brown, and David Morris—your presence is a steady force, a reminder that true friendship isn't just about weathering the storms, but also about appreciating the calm, the laughter, fun times, and the shared understanding that only comes with time.

Deep gratitude to the Wiley team for recognizing the vision of this book and bringing it to life through our partnership. Special shout out to Kelly Parisi who is the Godmother of this book.

When you are on the road 200 days a year, someone is keeping the home fires burning. To Janet Osimo—who is always there, always making the journey worth the homecoming. Thank you.

About the Author

Sylvia Acevedo | Author of *The Trailblazer's Playbook* Engineer, CEO, Strategist, Board Leader, Trailblazer.

Sylvia Acevedo is a boundary-breaking engineer and leadership strategist whose career spans space exploration, Silicon Valley, and C-suites. From working on missions at NASA's Jet Propulsion Laboratory to executive roles at Apple, Dell, and IBM, she's made a career of turning bold ideas into real-world results.

A trusted voice in tech, Sylvia serves on the boards of Qualcomm and Credo Technologies, where she is Lead Independent Director. She advises early-stage CEOs and has scaled companies from startup to successful exits—including co-founding REBA Technologies. As CEO of the Girl Scouts of the USA, she led the largest programmatic transformation in a century, with over 146 new badges in STEM, entrepreneurship, civics, and the outdoors—impacting millions.

Her influence extends beyond business. As a former White House Education Commissioner, she helped shape early childhood education policy at the federal level. She has been recognized by Forbes, Bloomberg, and InStyle and received Mexico's prestigious Ohtli Award and the Captain of Industry Leadership Award from IISE.

About the Author

Sylvia's best-selling memoir, *Path to the Stars*, inspired a generation. In *The Trailblazer's Playbook*, Sylvia Acevedo reveals the strategic mindset and decisive tactics that powered her rise—from NASA to the boardroom. Built around her Clarity–Courage–Conviction framework, this essential guide offers real-world insights drawn from bold leadership moves, high-stakes decisions, and the resilience forged through personal tragedy. For anyone ready to own their path, navigate complexity, and deliver meaningful results, this is your playbook.

Sylvia holds an engineering degree with honors from New Mexico State University and was one of the first Hispanics—male or female—to earn a graduate engineering degree from Stanford. She has received honorary doctorates from Duke University, Washington College, and Saint Mary's College.

Index

19th Amendment, passage (float commemoration), 167–168

A

Abilities
  meningitis, impact, 6–7
  proving, 34
Academic performance, stack-ranking, 8–9
Acevedo, Ofelia/Benito (meeting), 3
Achievements, 179
  boundaries, pushing, 30
Actions, 154
  impact, realization, 148
  weight, feeling (absence), 91
Adams, Howard, 27–28, 185
Ambitions
  perception, 31
  processing, absence, 92
  solitary pursuit, belief, 177
Amon, Cristiano, 181
Analytical skills, channeling, 49–50

Angelou, Maya, 135
Anger
  impact, 131
  powerlessness, relationship, 117
  presence, 90
  weight, 114–115
Ann Richards School for Young Women Leaders, 138
Apple, 49–54
Approval, desire, 10
Attention, commanding (importance), 87
Audience, captivity, 8
Authenticity, authority (balance), 47
Authority figures, relationships (issues), 90–91, 179
AutoCAD, power (showcasing), 97
Autodesk
  accomplishments, attention, 101–103
  career role, 95–99
Avon beauty products, selling, 19–20

B

Bank account, absence, 5
Barrier, breaking, 153
Blame, assigning (avoidance), 101
Board meetings, 183–184
Boundaries, pushing, 15
Boundary Taskforce, co-chairmanship, 136
Boy Scouts, 10–11
Brain damage, meningitis (impact), 6
Breathing exercises, usage, 119
Brennon, Bill, 182
Brewer, Kathrin, 139
Brown, Eric, 181–182
Burden, Stuart (advice), 145
Business
  growth, driving, 106
  sense, 98
  success, 135

C

Cal State Dominguez Hills, Univision (partnership), 144
Career
  defining strategy, 43
  long-term career, promise, 141
  progression, 105–106
  reshaping, 36
  roadmap, change, 81
Certificate of deposit (CD), opening/earnings, 5–6, 21–22
Change, requirements, 136–137, 144–145
Chaos, structure (sense), 74
Character, impact, 149

Children
  education, support, 143
  potential, barriers, 139–140
Cleveland, Genetha, 167–168
College, women attendance (myth), 41–42
Commitment, keeping, 54
Common ground, finding, 41, 55
Communication, 156–157
  failure, 105
  skills, 45–46, 85
Competence
  building, 14–15
  igniting, 163
Competing choice/ability, 14–15, 19
Comstock, Nora, 137
Confidence, 8, 26–27, 50, 83
  blow, 44
  building, 13
  igniting, 163
  persistence, 41
  projection, 46
  tempering, 101
  usage, 149
Connecting, importance, 87
Conviction, 54–57, 178
Corporate boards, serving, 184
Courage, 54–57
  dreams, impact, 30
  usage, 148
COVID-19, impact, 168
Creativity, 54–57
Credibility, building, 83
Credit card, absence, 5
Credo Technologies, 182

Curiosity, impact, 12–13
Customer Relationship Management (CRM), 50

D

Dawson, Susan, 139
Decision-making, importance, 41
Defiance, problem, 114
Deliberate practice, 20
Dell, 103–105
    contributions, communication (shift), 107–108
    feedback, 179–180
    goals, 108
    ideas, traction, 108
    job offer, 101–103
    long-term growth, 108
    performance, baseline, 106
Demographics, change, 140
Digital safety, understanding, 163
Dignity, restoration, 186
Discouragement, impact, 23
Distrust, focus, 115
Doubt
    appearance, 47
    weight, carrying, 122
Dreams
    abandonment, 22
    chasing/believing, 15
    chasing/building, 31, 56
    north star, 21
    power, 21
    pursuit, 42, 178
    realization, 185
Dual-language education, success, 147
Dynamic Signal, joining, 181–182

E

Economic growth, 135
Economic prosperity, graduation rates (impact), 140
Education
    economic opportunity, connection, 140–141
    system, navigation, 142
    emotional weight, avoidance, 84
Emotional weight, impact, 116–117
Emotions
    facing, 114
    flood, 121
Energy, channeling, 81
Enforcement, conversation (shift), 97
Engineer
    dream, pursuit, 42
    mold, women (myth), 42–43
Engineering
    curriculum, rigor, 33
    interest/seriousness, 24
    understanding, 26–27
Excellence
    commitment, 182
    importance, 86–87
Execution
    focus, 107
    relentlessness, 134–135
Executives
    buy-in, 108
    empathy, 75–76

F

Failure, 178
    consumption, 100
    impact, 109

Fall Seven Times, Stand Up Eight
  (proverb), 95
Family
  conversations, navigation, 116
  history, facing, 114
  legacy, loss, 124–125
Father
  understanding, 122–123
Father, memory (burying), 121
Fear, weight (carrying), 122
Feedback, 86–87, 179–180
  value, 35
Feria Para Aprender (The
    Learning Fair)
  Commitment Area, 143–144
  creation/design, 142–143
  STEM/robotics, 144
  Visualization Station, 143
Financial opportunity, creation,
    21–22
First Attempt In Learning
    (failure), 12
Forgione, Pat, 136
Forgiveness, struggle, 113, 126–127
Fragmented system, alignment, 141
Fulfillment (level), attainment
    (failure), 113
Future, defining, 180–181

G
GEM Fellowship, application,
    28–29
GEM Program, 27–28
General Motors (GM), 162
Generational trauma,
    recognition, 123

Girl Scout Research Institute
    (GSRI), 162
  council support team, training
    timeline (alignment),
    163–164
  programs, launch, 163
Girl Scouts of the USA
    (GSUSA), 148, 153
  accomplishments, 172
  badges, offering/expansion,
    161, 164
  CEO, role, 153–158, 180
  convention, 171–172
  Cookie Program, 165
  COVID-19, impact, 168
  cybersecurity badges, 165,
    172–173, 180
  essence, honoring, 162
  in-person cookie sales,
    cancellation, 169
  invitation, 10–11
  joining, 19
  leadership, 160–162
  legacy, 172–173
    building, 166–167
    stewardship, 171
  mobilization, 169–170
  movement, evolution, 167
  The North Face, partnership,
    163–164
  pivot, 169–170
  resilience, testament, 170–171
  Rose Bowl participation,
    167–168
  STEM badges/expansion, 164–166
  symbolism, value, 159–160

Girls, skills/confidence/vision (gain), 165–166
Global enterprise, infrastructure, 102
Goals
  importance, 22
  power, 41
  setting, 41
Goka, Jeanne, 137–138
Gordon Low, Juliette, 156
  legacy, continuation, 161
Governance, perspective, 182–183
Grace, extending, 122
Gratitude, 184–185
Grief
  carrying, 82
  processing, 92
  relentlessness/impact, 71–74
  resolution, absence, 90
Growth, 85
  daring, 20
  driving, 90, 106
  energy, channeling, 81
  openness, 178

H

Habit, formation, 132–133
Hall, Mike, 35–36
Head Start, impact, 145
Healing
  journey, 135
  time, need, 123
Honor, restoration, 186
Humor, restoration, 185–186
Hyper-vigilance, 118

I

IBM
  100% Club, attendance, 61
  colleagues
    sacrifices, 79
    support/compassion, 71–76
  culture, knowledge, 45
  design innovations, showcasing, 177–178
  executive empathy, 75–76
  mainframes, usage, 80
  manufacturing facility ceremony, 37
  mindset, understanding, 45
  sales culture, understanding, 45
  sales experience, 48–49
  Sales Training Program, 44–46
    position, availability, 48
  technological innovation, 42
  training programs, 61
  work, performance, 84
IBM, job, 34–37
Influence, importance, 88
Integrity, leadership, 182
International experience, chance, 50

J

Job
  creation, 140–141
  rejections, 44
Jobs, Steve (possibility message), 82
Journey, 187
  defining, failure (impact), 109
  transformation/resilience/hope, 178

L

Latin America
  black-market sales, 96
  market potential, 96–97
  piracy, presence, 95–96
Leaders
  communication, 82–83, 156–157
  credibility, defining, 100–101
  impact, 106
  response, problem, 100
Leadership
  building, 179
  courage/confidence/character, usage, 148–149
  earning, 157
  embodiment, 180
  independence, 115
  language, 106–107
  legacy, 172–173
  level, attainment (problems), 113
  meaning, 100–101
  Obama compliment, 148
  potential, unlocking, 172–173
  problem, 89–92
  roles, 81
  skill, learning, 109
  titles usage, limitations, 156–157, 178
Learning
  determination, 13
  importance, 15
  opportunity, 44
Legacy
  honoring, 160–161
  preservation, 153

Library card, usage, 4
  impact, 11–12
Life
  changes, 9
  contradictions, 125–126
Long-term career, promise, 141
Long-term goals, approach, 26
Long-term viability, 182
"Looking the part," 47
Loss
  sense, 70
  shame, 74
Love
  approval, search, 10
  expression, reluctance, 123
  testing, 7

M

Market share, success (relationship), 98
Math, language, 13–14
McCarthy, Kevin, 180
McLaughlin, Mark, 180–181
Meningitis, epidemic, 6
Mexico, currency (devaluation), 99–101
Mindset
  application, 140
  shift, 47
Model rocket, building, 11
Mother, understanding, 123–124

N

Narratives, connections, 125
NASA
  arrival, science badge/library card (usage/impact), 11–12

dreams, 61
job/work, 29, 34, 42, 87, 138, 164
   arrival, 30–32

O

Obama, Barack, 148
Obligations, weight, 19–20
Odierno, Ray, 147–148
Operational execution, expectation, 107
Opportunity
   creation, 19, 37, 41
   embracing, 132, 154
   long-term opportunities, 80–81
   missed opportunities, 91–92
   obstacles, relationship, 88–89
   seizing, 48
   transformation, 51–52
Outsider, feeling, 9–10
Overachievement, 114

P

Padrón, Eduardo, 146
Pain
   acknowledgment, 73
   fortress, building, 82–83, 116
   weight, carrying, 122
Palo Alto Networks, 162, 180
Parents
   divorce, possibility, 68–70
   funeral, 69–70, 72
   home, violence, 67–68
   loss, impact, 73–74, 179
   murder/suicide, 62–67
   problem, 7
   tragedy

kindness/strength, impact, 70–71
   survival, 71–72
   work, tirelessness, 19–20
Past, transformation, 127
Path to the Stars: My Journey from Girl Scout to Rocket Scientist, 153
Patience, exhaustion, 55–56
Performance, competing, 107
Perseverance, impact, 56
Persistence, 54–57
   impact, 12, 48
   payoff, uncertainty, 47
Personal mission, 43
Perspective, shift, 136
Posey, Lee/Sally, 137
Possibility
   impact, 131
   Jobs message, 82
   limitlessness, sense, 12–13
   sparking, 161
Post-Traumatic Stress Disorder (PTSD), 118
   therapist, assistance, 118–119
Potential, unlocking, 172–173
Power, holding, 172
Powerlessness, feeling, 117
Power users (Dell), impact, 104–105
Praise, expression (reluctance), 123
Presence
   focus, 88–89
   importance, 86–87
Problem-solving, 12–13, 22, 26–27, 134–135
   track record, 45–46

Product marketing, opportunity, 89
Professional excellence, 26–27
Professional growth, focus, 83–84
Progress
  meaning, 134
  pursuit, 148
Public policy, shaping, 132
Purpose
  expansion, 135
  impact, 149
  leadership, 182
  sense, renewal, 166–167

Q
Qualcomm, 181
Qualifications
  enthusiasm, disconnect, 53–54
  women, inability (myth), 49–52
Qualifications, impact, 23–24
Question, reframing, 42

R
Raytheon, 180, 162
Reality, collision, 34
Rejection, refusal, 44
Relationship-building, mastery, 49, 139
Resellers
  interaction, 97
  thriving, 98
Resilience
  impact, 126–127, 149, 178
  testament, 170–171, 185
  testing, 7
Resistance, 157
  resilience, contrast, 115
Resolve, testing, 22

Responsibilities, weight, 19–20
Revenue growth, success (relationship), 98
Richards, Ann, 136–137, 153
  leadership, 180
  vision, honoring, 137
Risk management, 182–183
Roadblocks, 134, 178
Rose Bowl, GSUSA float participation, 167–168
Rule of three nos, practice, 41–42

S
Saldaña, Hector (vision), 51
Sales, advice, 41
Salesforce, 162, 181
Sandia Labs, scholarship award/work, 24–26
San Jose Plant, IBM production facility (building), 35–36
Saving face, 32–33
Savings account, opening, 4–5
Scarcity, transformation, 124
Scholarship applications, 23–24
School
  after-school activities, 10
  grades, strength, 9–10
Science badge, impact, 11–12
Self-awareness, learning, 119–122
Self-belief, 3
Self-determination, 145
Self-doubt, 56, 92
Self-presentation, transformation (importance), 88
Self, reclaiming, 122–124
Self-reflection, 91

Senior executive leadership, language, 106–107
Setbacks
  navigation, 158
  reversal, 54–55
Shame
  burden, 116–117
  impact, 131
  weight, 74
Shelton, Jodi, 184
Silent agreement, 51
Skills, 145
  considerations, 46
  mastery, 14–15
Skillset, adaptation, 80–85
"Small job," 35
Social capital, 138–140
Solutions, focusing, 100–101
Stakeholders, emergence, 156
Stanford, 32–33
  attendance, 22–24, 27, 138
  GEM Program, 27–28
STEM concepts, 163
Storytelling
  learning, 82
  thrill, 8
  usage, 167
Strategic tasks, focus, 26
Strategic thinking, 134–135
Strategy
  perspective, 182
  shift, 136
Success
  detours/roadblocks, 56–57
  meaning, 14, 55–56, 106
    explanation, 26
  pursuit, 89–90, 177

  redefining, 134–135
  straight line, 131
  technical expertise, relationship, 81–82

T

Talent pipeline, 181
  problem, 135
Tan, Lip-Bu, 182
Teachers, importance, 8–10
Technological innovation (IBM), 42
Technology industry
  complexities, navigation, 49
  female leadership, Girl Scouts (relationship), 158
Tension, addressing, 90
Therapist, assistance, 117–122
Therapy, importance, 74
Thomas Branigan Library, usage, 4
Tiered pricing, introduction, 97
Tradition, continuation, 160–161
Tragedy, survival, 71–72
Trailblazer, resolve (acknowledgment), 51
Transformation, 36–37, 87–88, 164, 178
Trust
  building, 83, 110, 157–160
  earning, 139
  test, 154
Truth, reinforcement, 159

U

Uncertainty, change, 154
Underestimation, fight, 115
Unexpected, navigation (learning), 178

Unwritten rules, mastery, 47
Urgency
　importance, contrast, 25–27
　sense, creation, 142

V
Vigilance, anchoring, 116
Virtuous cycle, fueling, 13
Vision, shift, 137–138
Visualization, 31
Volunteering, 132–135
Vulnerability, 86, 114, 124

W
Weekly Reader, reading aloud, 9
White House Commission on Educational Excellence for Hispanics, 145–148
White House Education Commission, Early Childhood Subcommittee, 146
Women
　experience, need, 43
　young women, skills, 153
Words, flow, 9
Work
　control, 10
　energy, channeling, 82
　expansion, 131
　experience, need, 25–26
　hard work, impact, 36
　increase, push, 115
　mastery, 46
　roadmap, demands, 79–80
　structure/progress, 79
Workforce
　automation, 141
　digital skills, 162
　strengthening, 138–139
Worth, proof, 10
Written rules, mastery, 47

Y
Young Women's Prep Network, 137